PRIVATE
XXX
Preview
Booths

SWEAT

PRISCILLA
QUEEN OF THE DESERT
the musical

ronnie
scotts
6:20 pm - 3 am
OPEN NIGHT

ANDREA RIPLEY

GLASS CUPCAKE

GLASS STAND

BARGAIN
BOOKS

DEPT

DOWNSTAIRS

Kiss Me

Bite Me

Eat Me

COX COOKIES & CAKE

Eric Lanlard & Patrick Cox

COX COOKIES & CAKE

Eric Lanlard & Patrick Cox

First published in Great Britain in 2011 by Mitchell Beazley,
an imprint of Octopus Publishing Group Ltd,
Endeavour House, 189 Shaftesbury Avenue, London WC2H 8JY
www.octopusbooks.co.uk

An Hachette UK Company
www.hachette.co.uk

Distributed in the US by Hachette Book Group USA
237 Park Avenue, New York, NY 10017 USA
www.octopusbooksusa.com

Distributed in Canada by Canadian Manda Group
165 Dufferin Street, Toronto, Ontario, Canada M6K 3H6

Commissioning editor Becca Spry
Senior editor Sybella Stephens
Copy editor Lewis Esson
Proofreader Hilaire Walden
Indexer Ingrid Lock
Home economist Rachel Wood
Art director Jonathan Christie
Design & art direction Juliette Norsworthy
Photography Patrick Llewelyn-Davies & Johnnie Shand Kydd
Production manager Peter Hunt

ISBN: 978 1 84533 715 5
Printed and bound in China

Muffin-size cupcake pans and standard paper baking cups should be used for
all cupcake recipes, unless otherwise stated.
Medium eggs should be used, unless otherwise stated.
Whole milk should be used, unless otherwise stated.

CONTENTS

It was with a huge sense of wonderment and excitement when we first walked into the original Patrick Cox boutique on Symons Street in London. A velvet rope held back a wild throng of fashionistas, desperate to get their hands on a pair of his oh-so-hip Wannabe loafers. Cox's mad creativity and love of British irony transported the humble slip-on loafer and rocked it to the highest of heights. Mad candy colors, diamante embellishments, exotic animal skins, and pop culture detailing made Cox's loafers super-funky and unashamedly full-on fun.

After churning out millions of pairs of loafers and swirling stilettos, Cox has now boldly applied the same principles to an exciting range of deliriously delicious cakes. A long-time fan of homemade sweets—his mother Maureen has been mailing her delectable home-baked yummies to her beloved son in London from Canada for decades—he has now applied the same wit and irony to retail baking. Looking at a cupcake and cookie world festooned with gingham and butterflies, Cox decided to zig where others have zagged.

By commandeering a London Soho sex shop and teaming up with the baking genius of Eric Lanlard, who has made cakes for us for many years, Cox has virtually transformed the world of baked goods into an outrageously fun and delicious range of sinfully scrumptious madness.

Their Soho bakery has now become a must-see destination for the über-hip lover of indulgent sweeties with a funky vibe. Opening a box of Cox Cookies & Cake cupcakes puts the biggest smile on your face and transports you to a place where the worries of the day melt away into delicious mouthfuls of sinful fun and outrageous fabulousness. We love the cakes almost as much as we love our Patsy!

**SIR ELTON JOHN
& DAVID FURNISH**

FOREWORD

INTRODUCTION

I'm a designer. It's in my blood. It's who I am. It affects how I look at everything in the world. I see everyday objects, such as shoes, handbags, or cakes, and I want to make them sexier, inject them with glamor, and make them shine! For me life is the triumph of the fantastic over the dull, and when I saw the pastel-shaded world of cupcakes, I wanted to shake it up, sex it up, and create something breathtakingly new.

The result is Cox Cookies & Cake, a Soho bakery infused with seduction and style: the location in a former sex shop in the heart of London's historic redlight district; the original Tracey Emin neon piece on the wall; the staff in leather-studded aprons; the mirrored ceilings and the polished black floor—all come together to set the scene for the most dangerous thing to hit the world of cupcakes since self-rising flour.

However, at the heart of what I do are the cakes themselves. Here I faced my limitations as a designer. I needed a skilled pâtissier and business partner to make sure the cakes tasted every bit as good as they looked, with all the quality that one associates with the Patrick Cox name. Fortunately Elizabeth Hurley introduced me to world-renowned and fabulous Eric Lanlard (he made Elizabeth's wedding cake) and as soon as we met I knew instantly we could work together and make the vision of Cox Cookies & Cake a reality.

Together we've created cakes that are sexy, unbelievably tasty, and fun. They pay homage to sex, art, fashion, and even politics. Each cake is like a work of art, yet unlike some of the shoes I used to make or Warhol paintings, our cakes are affordable and available for everyone.

This book takes that accessibility further. I want people to enjoy the design process themselves, have fun creating these cakes at home, and see the same joy I see every day on the faces of my customers and in the reactions of their families and friends. So turn on the music, crank up the volume, and get baking…Cox Cookies & Cake style!

PATRICK COX

I'm a pâtissier. It's in my blood and who I am, or at least who I have been since I was a little boy staring in the windows of my local pâtisserie. In times where form often triumphs over substance and where looks too often succeed over taste, it has always been my mission to make cakes that taste as good as they look; cakes where the feasting of the eyes is not followed by a bite of disappointment, but by a feasting of the taste buds. I have been putting this philosophy into practice within my own business over the past 16 years, and with Cox Cookies & Cake I now have a new outlet for my naughtier skills.

Before having the pleasure of meeting Patrick, glamor was always very much part of my world, reflected in the title of my first book *Glamour Cakes* and my first two TV series' *Glamour Puds*. As an artisan I've always used cake design as my creative outlet. However, nothing had prepared me for the excitement I felt on first hearing about Patrick's vision, pushing my boundaries way beyond anything I would have dared to do myself.

The results of our efforts speak for themselves in the happy faces of our customers in the wonderful shop that Patrick has designed in the heart of Soho life. I hope this book enables you to bake a little of this excitement in your own home and put happy faces on your friends and family alike.

ERIC LANLARD

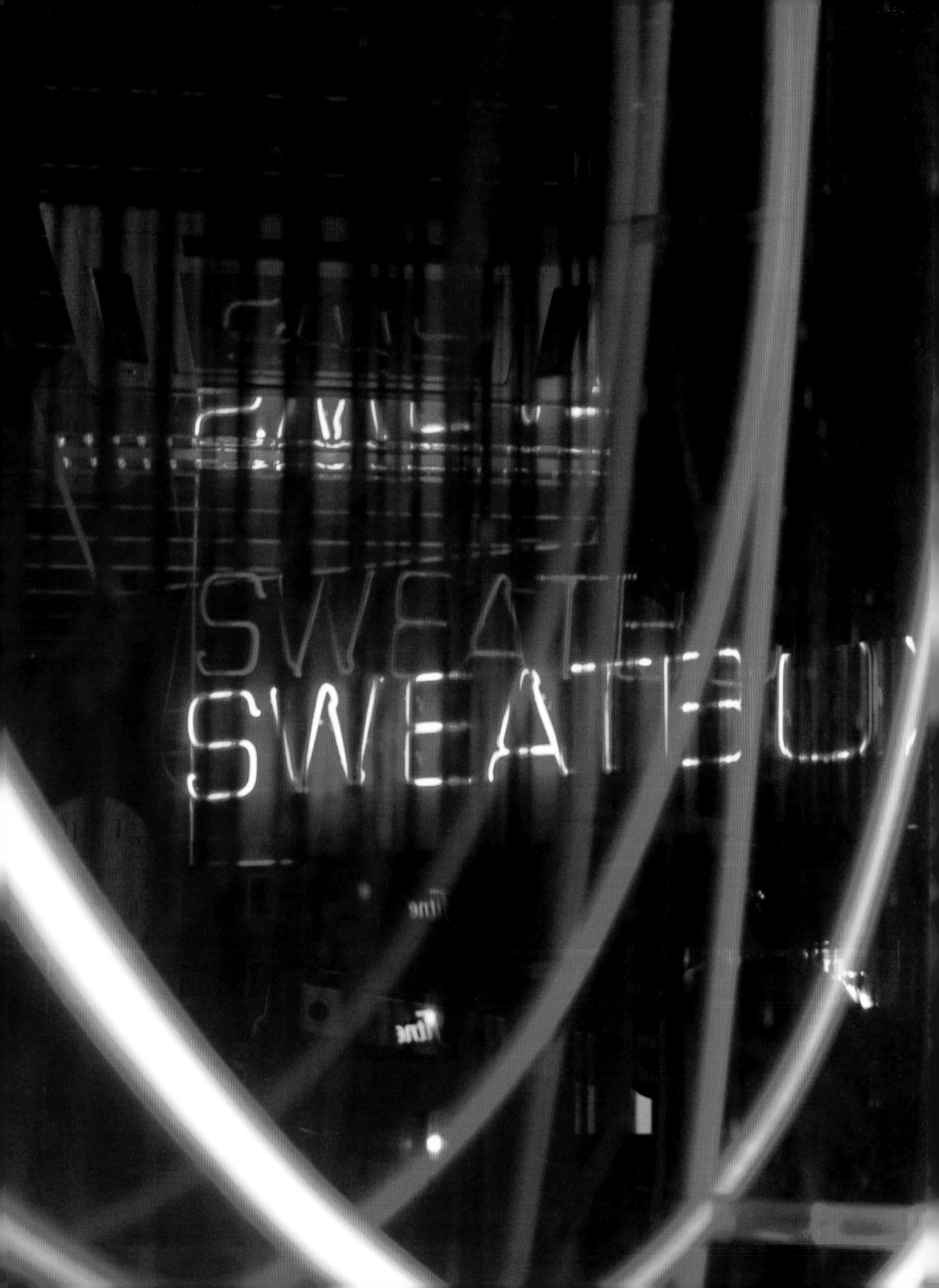

1

Put some fizz into your cupcakes! These little miracles will delight kids and adults, too. The cola makes the cake light and airy, and the addition of the popping candy on top makes them a truly fun experience.

COLA CUPCAKES

MAKES 12 CUPCAKES

1¾ sticks unsalted butter
1 cup cola (I prefer to use the old-fashioned original one because it has more flavor)
2 cups self-rising flour
1 tsp baking powder
1 tbsp unsweetened cocoa powder
1 cup superfine sugar
2 eggs, beaten
⅔ cup milk

FOR THE COLA FROSTING

7 tbsp unsalted butter, softened
¼ cup unsweetened cocoa powder
3¾ cups confectioner's sugar
scant ½ cup cola
1 tsp vanilla extract
cola-flavored popping candy or fizzy cola bottles, to decorate

Preheat the oven to 400°F, and line a cupcake pan with paper baking cups.

In a saucepan, gently heat the butter and cola until the butter has melted. Remove from the heat and leave to cool.

Sift the flour, baking powder, and cocoa powder together. Add the cooled cola and butter mixture, followed by the sugar and eggs. Mix together then add just enough milk a little at a time until the mixture is smooth.

Divide the batter between the baking cups. Bake for 25–30 minutes, or until a skewer inserted into the center of a cupcake comes out clean. Leave to cool in the pan for 5 minutes then transfer to a wire rack and allow to cool completely before frosting.

To make the Cola Frosting: cream the butter in a bowl. Sift the cocoa and confectioner's sugar together and mix into the butter a little at a time, alternating with additions of the cola. Beat to give a nice smooth frosting. (You may need to add more cola if the frosting is too stiff). Beat in the vanilla extract.

Pipe the frosting onto the cooled cupcakes and decorate with either popping candy or fizzy cola bottles.

This now-celebrated cupcake is usually made as a large cake and there are many variations, including some that use beet juice to give the rich red color. In this recipe I use a combination of pure unsweetened cocoa powder, vinegar, and red food coloring to achieve a vibrant tone.

RED VELVET CUPCAKES

MAKES 12 CUPCAKES

¼ cup + 1 tbsp unsweetened
   cocoa powder
1 tsp vanilla extract
5 tbsp unsalted butter, softened
heaped ¾ cup superfine sugar
2 egg yolks
pinch of salt
²/₃ cup buttermilk
1¼ cups all-purpose flour, sifted
½ tsp baking soda
½ tsp white wine vinegar
1 tsp red food coloring

FOR THE FROSTING

½ cup milk
1½ tbsp all-purpose flour
pinch of salt
7 tbsp unsalted butter, softened
1½ cups confectioner's sugar, plus
   extra for dusting
3½oz white chocolate, melted
   and cooled
½ tsp vanilla extract

Preheat the oven to 400°C, and line a cupcake pan with paper baking cups.

In a small bowl, combine the cocoa powder and vanilla extract. Set aside.

In a large bowl, beat the butter and sugar together using a stand mixer or an electric hand mixer on medium-high speed. Add the yolks. Beat for another minute then add the cocoa mixture.

Stir the salt into the buttermilk. Mix one-third into the butter mixture, followed by one-third of the flour. Repeat with two further batches of each until all are mixed in.

Mix the baking soda with the vinegar and blend this, along with the food coloring, into the batter. Divide the batter between the baking cups. Bake for 20–25 minutes, or until a skewer inserted into the center of a cupcake comes out clean.

Allow the cupcakes to cool in the pan for 10 minutes. Then remove the cupcakes from the pan and allow to cool completely before frosting.

To make the frosting: in a small saucepan, whisk the milk, flour, and salt over medium heat for 1 or 2 minutes until the mixture thickens and begins to bubble. Transfer to a small bowl and leave to cool.

Beat the butter and confectioner's sugar together until light and fluffy. Stir in the cooled chocolate, the milk mixture, and the vanilla extract, and mix until smooth and fluffy.

Spread or pipe the frosting onto the cooled cupcakes. Crumble some baked red sponge cake on top (you may have to sacrifice one of your cupcakes). Dust with confectioner's sugar to finish.

Here's one for the chocoholics! There's cocoa powder, melted chocolate, and chocolate chips in this beautiful moist cupcake. Then, for a rich finish, it's covered with chocolate frosting and a coating of chocolate sprinkles. Heaven!

TRIPLE CHOCOLATE CUPCAKES

MAKES 12 CUPCAKES

3oz semisweet chocolate, broken into pieces
1¾ sticks unsalted butter
1 heaped cup superfine sugar
3 eggs
½ tsp baking powder
1⅓ cups all-purpose flour
¼ cup unsweetened cocoa powder
heaped ¼ cup semisweet chocolate chips
1 quantity Chocolate Frosting (see page 91)
mixture of mini white, milk, and dark chocolate sprinkles, to decorate

Preheat the oven to 400°F, and line a cupcake pan with paper baking cups.

In a large saucepan, melt the chocolate and butter over medium heat, stirring to prevent if from burning. Allow this to cool for a few minutes.

Stir in the sugar until well mixed. Add the eggs, one at a time, until you have a smooth batter. Sift the baking powder, flour, and cocoa powder into the batter and mix until smooth. Then fold in the chocolate chips.

Divide the batter between the paper baking cups to just about three-quarters full—don't overfill them. Bake for 20–25 minutes, or until a skewer inserted into the center of a cupcake comes out clean.

Leave to cool in the pan for 5 minutes then transfer to a wire rack and allow to cool completely before frosting. I like to spread Chocolate Frosting on top of the cupcakes and then cover them with mini chocolate sprinkles to decorate.

We call this classic the Irish cupcake because of the addition of Irish cream liqueur, which works perfectly with the chocolate base. Kids should be kept well away from these!

IRISH CREAM & CHOCOLATE CUPCAKES

MAKES 12 CUPCAKES

3oz semisweet chocolate, plus
    extra for decorating
1¾ sticks unsalted butter
1 heaped cup superfine sugar
1 tsp vanilla extract
1 tbsp of Irish cream liqueur
3 eggs
¼ cup unsweetened cocoa powder
1⅓ cups all-purpose flour
½ tsp baking powder
chocolate curls, to decorate

FOR THE FROSTING

2 sticks unsalted butter
3oz semisweet chocolate,
    melted and cooled
4½ cups confectioner's sugar
3 tbsp Irish cream liqueur

Preheat the oven to 400°F, and line a cupcake pan with paper baking cups.

Add the chocolate and butter to a large heatproof bowl and set it over a saucepan of barely simmering water, making sure the bowl does not touch the surface of the water. Stir until completely melted then remove from the heat. Stir in the sugar, vanilla extract, and Irish cream liqueur.

Beat in the eggs one at a time. Sift in the cocoa powder, flour, and baking powder and combine until smooth.

Spoon the mixture into the baking cups, filling each three-quarters full. Bake for 20–25 minutes, or until a skewer inserted into the center of a cupcake comes out clean.

Leave to cool in the pan for 5 minutes then transfer to a wire rack and allow to cool completely before covering with frosting.

To make the frosting: beat the butter into the melted chocolate until smooth. Gradually beat in the confectioner's sugar and finally add the Irish cream liqueur. Using a small metal spatula, spread the frosting over the cupcakes or pipe it on in spirals. Decorate with chocolate curls.

If you are a fan of Mounds chocolate bars, these cupcakes are for you. Coated with a rich cinnamon ganache, they have a true taste of paradise.

CHOCOLATE & COCONUT CUPCAKES

MAKES 12 CUPCAKES

1 cup superfine sugar
1¾ sticks unsalted butter, softened
3 eggs
3 tbsp milk
1⅓ cups self-rising flour
½ tsp baking powder
heaped ¾ cup desiccated coconut

FOR THE CHOCOLATE GANACHE

5oz semisweet chocolate
    (55% cocoa solids), broken
    into small pieces
⅔ cup heavy cream
3½ tbsp very soft unsalted butter
1 tsp ground cinnamon
toasted desiccated coconut, to
    decorate

Preheat the oven to 400°F, and line a cupcake pan with paper baking cups.

In a large bowl, cream the sugar and butter together until pale and fluffy using a stand mixer or an electric hand mixer, then stir in the eggs one at a time, followed by the milk. Beat until everything is well incorporated.

Fold the flour and baking powder into butter mixture until smooth and well combined. Finally fold in the coconut.

Divide the batter between the paper baking cups. Bake for 20 minutes or until a skewer inserted into the center of a cupcake comes out clean. Leave to cool in the pan for 5 minutes, then transfer to a wire rack to cool completely.

To make the Chocolate Ganache: add the chocolate to a medium-sized bowl. Put the cream in a small saucepan over medium heat and, as soon as it reaches boiling point, pour it over the chocolate. Leave this to stand until the chocolate pieces have melted.

Once they have melted, pass the mixture through a sieve into a bowl. Then stir in the softened butter and cinnamon. Leave to cool and set slightly.

As soon as the mixture has set, beat it in a stand mixer or using an electric hand mixer until it has almost doubled in volume.

Spread the ganache over the cooled cupcakes then scatter with toasted desiccated coconut to decorate.

The rich semisweet chocolate batter and the sweetness of the raspberries is a combination made in heaven. Then, with a chocolate frosting and more fresh raspberries on top…yummy!

CHOCOLATE & RASPBERRY CUPCAKES

MAKES 12 CUPCAKES

1⅛ sticks unsalted butter

3oz semisweet chocolate, broken into large pieces

1 tsp instant coffee

1 tsp vanilla extract

¾ cup light soft brown sugar

2 eggs, lightly beaten

1 tsp baking powder

1¾ cups self-rising flour

⅔ cup water

3⅔ cups raspberries, plus extra to decorate

1 quantity Chocolate Frosting (see page 91)

Preheat the oven to 400°F, and line a cupcake pan with paper baking cups.

Melt the butter in a large heatproof bowl placed over a saucepan of barely simmering water, making sure the bowl does not touch the surface of the water. When it is half melted, add the chocolate. When the chocolate has melted completely remove from the heat and stir to blend in any lumps. Allow to cool for a few minutes.

Dissolve the coffee in the vanilla extract, then stir this mixture, along with the brown sugar, into the cooled chocolate and butter. When they are fully blended in, stir in the eggs and combine.

Sift the baking powder and the flour into the mixture and beat until all ingredients are well incorporated and the batter is thick. Then stir in the water a little at a time, making sure the liquid is completely absorbed into the batter.

Divide the batter between the paper baking cups, filling each about half full. Place 3 raspberries on the surface of each—they will sink into the batter. Then fill each cup almost to the top and place another fresh raspberry on top.

Bake for about 25 minutes, or until each cupcake is firm to touch or a skewer inserted into the center of a cupcake comes out clean. Leave to cool in the pan for 10 minutes and then transfer to a wire rack to cool completely. Once cool, pipe Chocolate Frosting in swirls on top of each cupcake and decorate with fresh raspberries.

Don't be discouraged by the lengthy preparation needed for this recipe—all the effort is well worth it to make these very tasty grown-up cupcakes. I like using Amarena cherries if I can get them—Italian delis often stock them.

BLACK FOREST CUPCAKES

MAKES 12 CUPCAKES

14oz jar or can of pitted black
   cherries in syrup, drained
   (reserving the syrup)
3½oz semisweet chocolate
   (50% cocoa solids), broken
   into pieces
1½ sticks unsalted butter,
   roughly cubed
1½ cups superfine sugar
4 tbsp cherry brandy
1¼ cups all-purpose flour, sifted
2 tbsp self-rising flour, sifted
2 tbsp unsweetened cocoa powder
1 egg

FOR THE DECORATION

2 tsp cherry brandy
generous ¾ cup heavy cream
2oz chunk of semisweet chocolate
   (50% cocoa solids), optional

Preheat the oven to 400°F, and line a cupcake pan with paper bakiing cups.

Put a generous ⅓ cup of the cherries and ½ cup of their syrup in a food processor and process until it becomes a smooth puree.

Cut the remaining cherries in half and reserve the rest of the syrup.

Place the cherry puree in a saucepan together with the chocolate, butter, sugar, and cherry brandy. Stir over low heat until the chocolate has melted. Pour into a large bowl and allow to cool for 15 minutes.

When cool, whisk in the flours and the cocoa powder, followed by the egg. It will be very runny, but that is OK.

Divide the batter between the paper baking cups. You will probably find that you fill the baking cups close to the top, but do not worry—the cupcakes will not rise a great deal.

Bake for 40–45 minutes, or until firm to touch or a skewer inserted into the center of a cupcake comes out clean. Allow to cool in the pan for 5 minutes then transfer to a wire rack to cool completely.

To decorate, mix the cherry brandy into the remaining cherry halves. Whip the cream to soft peaks, and pipe swirls on top of each cake.

Place some of the brandy-soaked cherry halves onto each cupcake and drizzle the reserved syrup on top. If using, scrape along the side of the chocolate chunk with a vegetable peeler to create curls and use these to decorate the top of each cupcake.

For this recipe I use a mixture of mini marshmallows and marshmallow creme to frost a rich and gooey brownie-like cupcake. The marshmallow creme gives these devilish little cupcakes a fun, toasted-marshmallow dimension, along with an extra marshmallow hit!

CHOCOLATE & MARSHMALLOW CUPCAKES

MAKES 12 CUPCAKES

3oz semisweet chocolate, broken
  into pieces
1¾ sticks unsalted butter
1 heaped cup superfine sugar
3 eggs
½ tsp baking powder
¼ cup unsweetened cocoa powder
1⅓ cups all-purpose flour
confectioner's sugar, to decorate

FOR THE MARSHMALLOW BUTTERCREAM FROSTING
2¼ sticks unsalted butter, softened
1 heaped cup marshmallow creme,
  plus extra to decorate
mini marshmallows, to decorate
  (optional)

Preheat the oven to 400°F, and line a cupcake pan with paper baking cups.

In a large saucepan over medium heat, melt the chocolate and butter, stirring constantly to stop it from burning. Allow to cool for a few minutes, then add the sugar and stir until well mixed.

Add the eggs, one at a time, until you have a smooth mixture. Then sift in the baking powder, flour, and cocoa powder and mix just until smooth.

Divide the batter between the paper baking cups filling them about three-quarters full—don't overfill them. Bake for 20–25 minutes, or until a skewer inserted into the center of a cupcake comes out clean. Leave to cool in the pan for 10 minutes and then transfer to a wire rack to cool completely.

To make the Marshmallow Buttercream Frosting: beat the butter and marshmallow creme together until smooth. Using a small metal spatula, spread the frosting on top of the cupcakes. If you want to add an extra marshmallow hit, spoon a couple of teaspoons of creme on top of the frosting, add some mini marshmallows, if liked, and dust with confectioner's sugar to finish.

Beware! The marshmallow creme will drip down the frosting, so don't let these cakes hang around for too long (although I love the way they look when this happens).

What makes this banana cupcake special is the roasting of the banana—its flavor becomes much more intense and sweet. You can decorate these with a classic Vanilla Buttercream Frosting, but I like eating them while still warm served with vanilla ice cream.

BANANA WALNUT CUPCAKES

MAKES 12 CUPCAKES

¾ cup walnuts, roughly chopped, plus extra to decorate (optional)

3 soft medium-sized bananas, peeled and sliced

½ cup soft dark brown sugar

1 tsp grated nutmeg

1³/₈ sticks unsalted butter, softened

¾ cup soft brown sugar

4 eggs, lightly beaten

1 cup self-rising whole-wheat flour

½ tsp baking powder

1 quantity Vanilla Buttercream Frosting (see page 88)

Preheat the oven to 400°F, and line a cupcake pan with paper baking cups.

Place the walnuts on a cookie sheet and toast in the oven for 5 minutes, making sure they do not burn. Set aside to cool.

Place the banana slices on a large piece of foil. Sprinkle with the dark brown sugar and then the nutmeg. Wrap the foil around the banana mixture and bake for 20–25 minutes, or until soft and mushy. Set aside to cool.

In a large bowl, cream the butter and soft brown sugar until light and fluffy, then gradually beat in the eggs. Sift the flour and baking powder and fold them into the mixture.

Once the bananas have cooled, place a sieve over a bowl and put the banana mixture carefully into the sieve. Discard the sugary liquid that drains into the bowl and add the banana slices remaining in the sieve to a clean bowl. Mash them, then fold them, along with the chopped walnuts, into the batter.

Divide the batter between the paper baking cups. Bake for 20–25 minutes, or until a skewer inserted into the center of a cupcake comes out clean.

These are great served warm with ice cream. Or, as an alternative, spread the cupcakes with Vanilla Buttercream Frosting then scatter with some chopped walnuts to finish.

This recipe uses very soft coconut sponge cake with an indulgent mascarpone cheese frosting. I like using long strands of dry coconut for the topping. To spoil yourself, try drizzling some melted semisweet chocolate on top of the cupcakes. This recipe can be made very grown-up by the addition of some Malibu coconut liqueur.

COCONUT CUPCAKES

MAKES 12 CUPCAKES

1½ sticks unsalted butter, softened
²/₃ cup superfine sugar
3 eggs, beaten
3 tbsp unsweetened cocoa powder
heaped ½ cup desiccated coconut
1¼ cups all-purpose flour
1 tsp baking powder
¼ cup milk

FOR THE FROSTING

1¹/₃ cup mascarpone cheese
½ cup confectioner's sugar
zest of 1 lime
heaped ½ cup desiccated coconut
²/₃ cup thin strands of fresh
    coconut, toasted

Preheat the oven to 400°F, and line a cupcake pan with paper baking cups.

In a large bowl, cream together the butter and sugar until pale and light. Add the beaten eggs and mix well. Add the cocoa powder and coconut, and mix in well. Sift the flour and baking powder together and then fold it into he butter and egg mixture. Add the milk and mix until smooth.

Divide the batter between the paper baking cups and bake on the middle rack of the oven for 20 minutes, or until the cakes are golden and a skewer inserted into the center of a cupcake comes out clean. Leave to cool in the pan for 5 minutes and then transfer to a wire rack to cool completely.

To make the frosting: beat the mascarpone cheese, confectioner's sugar, and lime zest together until smooth. Add the desiccated coconut and mix in well. When ready, spread an even layer of the frosting on top of each cupcake. Scatter with toasted coconut strands, to finish.

Here are all the flavors of the Middle East in a cute little cupcake—the combination of the spices, floral extracts, and nuts works so well. I like to scatter dried organic rose petals on top of mine.

PISTACHIO & ROSEWATER CUPCAKES

MAKES 12 CUPCAKES

½ cup plain yogurt
⅔ cup milk
¼ cup + 1 tbsp sunflower oil
heaped ¾ cup superfine sugar
1½ tbsp rosewater
1⅓ cups all-purpose flour
2 tbsp cornstarch
½ tsp baking soda
½ tsp baking powder
1 tsp vanilla extract
generous pinch of cardamom
    seeds (the little black seeds
    inside cardamom pods)
scant ½ cup chopped pistachio nuts

FOR THE ROSEWATER GLAZE
1⅔ cups confectioner's sugar
1 tbsp unsalted butter
2–3 tsp milk
½ tsp rosewater

Preheat the oven to 400°F, and line a cupcake pan with paper baking cups.

In a large bowl, beat together the yogurt, milk, oil, sugar, and rosewater. Sift in the flour, cornstarch, baking soda, and baking powder, then stir in the vanilla extract, cardamom seeds, and chopped pistachio nuts.

Divide the mixture between the paper baking cups, but only fill them three-quarters full. Bake for 20–25 minutes, or until a skewer inserted into the center of a cupcake comes out clean.

Leave to cool in the pan for 5 minutes and then transfer to a wire rack to cool completely before covering with the rosewater glaze.

To make the Rosewater Glaze: cut all of the butter into half of the confectioner's sugar until the mixture resembles fine crumbs, then mix in the milk and rosewater. Finally beat in the remaining confectioner's sugar. Spread the glaze on top of the cupcakes to finish.

These little marvels are so irresistible, with a pistachio sponge cake topped with Italian meringue and nutty praline. They also look very pretty, with the praline shining like jewels.

PISTACHIO & PRALINE CUPCAKES

MAKES 12 CUPCAKES

1⅛ sticks unsalted butter, softened
heaped ¾ cup superfine sugar
seeds from ½ vanilla bean
⅓ cup pistachio nut paste
2 eggs
1½ cups all-purpose flour
1 tsp baking powder
½ cup milk

FOR THE PISTACHIO PRALINE
sunflower oil, for brushing
⅔ cup unsalted pistachio nuts
1 cup superfine sugar
½ cup water

FOR THE MERINGUE TOPPING
¾ cup superfine sugar
3 tbsp water
generous pinch of cream of tartar
2 egg whites
pinch of salt

Preheat the oven to 400°F, and line a cupcake pan with paper baking cups.

Beat together the butter, sugar, vanilla seeds, and pistachio nut paste until light and creamy. Slowy add the eggs and beat again. Sift in the flour and baking powder, and beat until combined. Stir in the milk. Divide the batter between the baking cups. Bake for 15–17 minutes, or until a skewer inserted into the center of a cupcake comes out clean. Remove the cupcakes from the pan and transfer them to a wire rack to cool.

To make the Pistachio Praline: line a baking pan with foil, brush it with sunflower oil, and scatter the nuts onto the foil. Place the sugar and water in a saucepan over low heat, stirring until the sugar has dissolved. Increase the heat and bring to a boil, brushing any sugar crystals down the inside of the pan with a wet pastry brush. Cook for 8–10 minutes, or until dark golden. Remove from the heat and pour onto the nuts. Leave to cool, then chop into small chunks.

To make the Meringue Topping: combine the sugar, water, and cream of tartar in a heavy saucepan on medium heat and stir until it boils. Insert a candy thermometer. When the syrup reaches 230°F, whisk the egg whites, ideally in a stand mixer, until stiff. When the syrup reaches 250°F, with the mixer still on, slowly pour the syrup into the egg whites down the side of the bowl avoiding the whisk. Beat until the meringue is thick, glossy, and completely cold, about 10–15 minutes. To decorate, pipe the meringue onto the cupcakes (see page 98 for styling tips). Arrange a few nuggets of pistachio praline on top.

This all-American classic is such a versatile recipe. It is usually made as a loaf, a round, or baked in a square pan—but now as cupcakes! Using oil instead of butter as a fat gives you a very moist result. The cream cheese frosting is rich and delicious, but make sure you use a very dry cream cheese to get a nice firm texture. These cupcakes will keep very well in a pan, but do not store them in the fridge because they will go hard.

CARROT CAKE CUPCAKES

MAKES 12 CUPCAKES

1 cup sunflower or corn oil
1 heaped cup golden superfine sugar
3 eggs
1¾ cups self-rising flour
1 tsp ground cinnamon
1 tsp ground nutmeg
1²/₃ cups carrots, coarsely grated
heaped ¾ cup golden raisins, plus extra to decorate
heaped ¾ cup chopped walnuts, plus extra to decorate

FOR THE CREAM CHEESE FROSTING

1 scant cup reduced-fat cream cheese
1 cup unrefined golden confectioner's sugar, sifted
finely grated zest of 1 orange

Preheat the oven to 400°F, and line a cupcake pan with paper baking cups.

Pour the oil into a large bowl, add the superfine sugar, and beat with a large whisk for a few minutes. Then add the eggs one at a time.

Sift the flour, cinnamon, and nutmeg together, and, using a large metal spoon, fold the flour mixture into the egg mixture. Then fold in the carrots, golden raisins, and walnuts.

Divide the batter between the paper baking cups and bake for 20 minutes, or until a skewer inserted into the center of a cupcake comes out clean. Leave to cool in the pan for 5 minutes and then transfer to a wire rack to cool completely.

To make the Cream Cheese Frosting: gently beat the cream cheese until it is soft and smooth. Then gradually add the confectioner's sugar, followed by the orange zest.

When the cupcakes are cold, use a small metal spatula to spread the frosting on the top of each cake. Decorate each one with few golden raisins and some chopped walnuts.

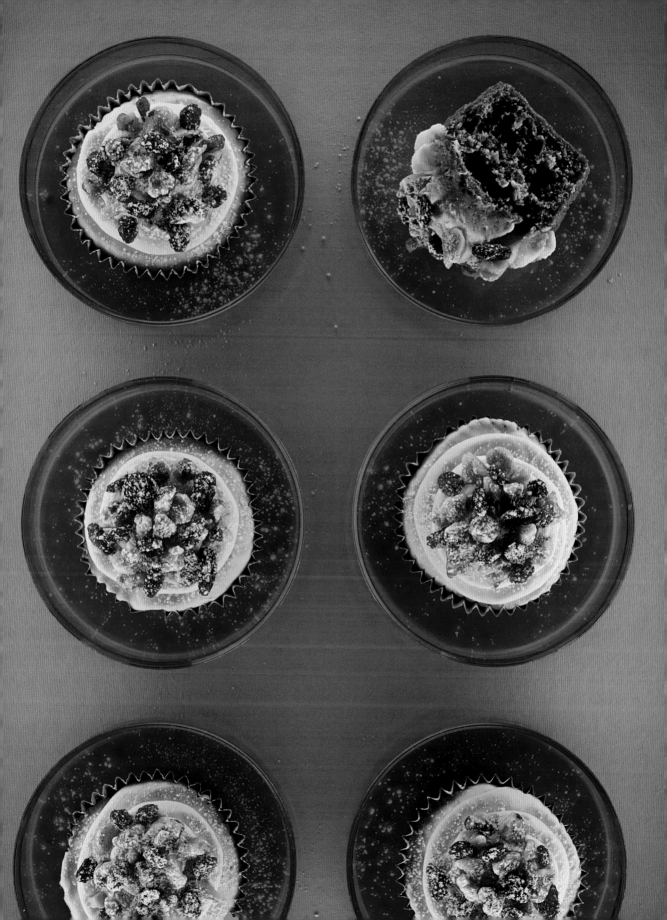

These cupcakes are just so delicious; the combination of the rich chocolate and the salty, crunchy peanut butter works wonderfully.

CHOCOLATE PEANUT BUTTER CUPCAKES

MAKES 12 CUPCAKES

1½ sticks unsalted butter
¾ cup superfine sugar
¾ cup light brown sugar
2 eggs
2 tsp vanilla extract
1 cup buttermilk
½ cup sour cream
2 tbsp espresso coffee
2 tbsp crunchy peanut butter
2 cups all-purpose flour
1 cup unsweetened cocoa powder
1½ tsp baking powder

FOR THE PEANUT BUTTER FROSTING

1¼ cups confectioner's sugar
½ cup smooth peanut butter
3½ tbsp unsalted butter, softened
¾ tsp vanilla extract
2 tbsp heavy cream
chopped salted peanuts, to
    decorate

Preheat the oven to 400°F, and line a cupcake pan with paper baking cups.

Cream the butter with both sugars, ideally in the bowl of a stand mixer or using an electric hand mixer, on high speed until light and fluffy (about 5 minutes). Lower the speed to medium, and add the eggs one at a time. Then add the vanilla extract and mix in well.

In another bowl, whisk together the buttermilk, sour cream, coffee, and peanut butter.

Into a third bowl, sift together the flour, cocoa powder, and baking powder.

On low speed, add one-third of the buttermilk mixture followed by one-third of the flour mixture to the butter and sugar mixture, beating only until just blended. Repeat until all the buttermilk and flour have been incorporated. Gently fold the batter with a spatula to ensure everything is completely blended. Divide the batter between the baking cups. Bake for 20–25 minutes, or until a skewer inserted into the center of a cupcake comes out clean. Leave to cool in the pan for 5 minutes, then transfer to a wire rack to cool completely.

To make the Peanut Butter Frosting: mix the confectioner's sugar, peanut butter, butter, and vanilla extract in a stand mixer on medium-low speed (or use an electric hand mixer) until creamy, scraping down the bowl with a spatula as you work. Add the cream and beat on high speed until the mixture is light and smooth. Using a pastry bag fitted with a small round tip, pipe the frosting onto each cupcake (see page 98 for styling tips). Finish by scattering the frosted cupcakes with chopped salted peanuts.

CENSED
X SHOP
SEMENT

2

These fresh, zesty cupcakes make great summer treats. You could add some chopped fresh mint to turn them into Mojito cupcakes, and a cup of roasted coconut in the mix works very well, too. Its a good idea to make the crystallized lime zest decoration the day before you want to serve these cupcakes.

KEY LIME CUPCAKES

MAKES 12 CUPCAKES

1½ sticks unsalted butter, softened
1½ cups superfine sugar
3 eggs
finely grated zest of 1 lime and
    4 tbsp juice
1 tsp vanilla extract
2½ cups all-purpose flour
1 tsp baking powder
1½ cups buttermilk

FOR THE CRYSTALLIZED LIME ZEST

2 unwaxed limes
½ cup superfine sugar, plus extra
    to coat
scant ½ cup water

FOR THE LIME SYRUP

¼ cup confectioner's sugar
    dissolved in the juice of 1½ limes

FOR THE WHITE CHOCOLATE FROSTING

7oz white chocolate, broken into
    pieces
½ cup heavy cream
1½ sticks unsalted butter, softened
grated zest of 1 lime and juice of ½
3 cups confectioner's sugar

To make the Crystallized Lime Zest: pare the zest from each lime, then carefully cut it into thin strips. Add the superfine sugar and the water to a pan and bring to a boil, stirring. Once bubbling, add one-third of the lime zest and cook for 3–4 minutes. Remove the zest, roll gently in superfine sugar, and set on waxed paper. (Space the pieces of zest out or they will stick together in clumps.) Repeat with the remaining zest and leave to dry overnight.

Preheat the oven to 400°F, and line a cupcake pan with paper baking cups.

Using a stand mixer or an electric hand mixer, cream the butter and sugar until pale and fluffy. Slowly beat in the eggs, one at the time. Add the lime zest and juice, then the vanilla extract. In another bowl, sift together the flour and baking powder. Gradually add this to the butter mixture with alternate spoonfuls of buttermilk. Divide the batter between the baking cups. Bake for 25–30 minutes, or until a skewer inserted into the center of a cupcake comes out clean. Leave to cool in the pans for 5 minutes then transfer to a wire rack. While warm, use a toothpick to prick small holes into the top of each cupcake. Drizzle a teaspoon of lime syrup over each and allow it to soak and cool before frosting.

To make the frosting: melt the chocolate with the cream in a heatproof bowl set over a saucepan of simmering water, making sure the bowl does not touch the surface of the water. Allow the chocolate to cool completely. Then whisk in the butter, lime zest, juice, and confectioner's sugar. When smooth, use a pastry bag to pipe the frosting onto each cupcake, and decorate with a few strands of crystallized lime zest.

This light and zesty cupcake carries off the rich white chocolate frosting with serious style, making a great summer dessert. Lemon curd is available by mail order online and in gourmet markets and some supermarkets.

ZESTY LEMON & WHITE CHOCOLATE CUPCAKES

MAKES 12 CUPCAKES

1½ sticks unsalted butter, softened
½ cup superfine sugar
2 eggs
1 scant cup plain yogurt
grated zest of 1 lemon and
    2 tsp lemon juice
½ tsp lemon oil
1½ cups all-purpose flour
1 tsp baking powder
2 tsp poppy seeds
½ of an 11oz jar of lemon curd

FOR THE WHITE CHOCOLATE FROSTING

5 tbsp unsalted butter
¼ cup + 1 tbsp cream cheese
1¼ cups confectioner's sugar
3½oz white chocolate, melted, plus
    extra to decorate

Preheat the oven to 400°F, and line a cupcake pan with paper baking cups.

In a large bowl, cream the butter and sugar together until light and fluffy. Then mix in the eggs, one at a time, followed by the yogurt, lemon zest and juice, and the lemon oil. Sift the flour and baking powder together and stir this into the butter mixture with the poppy seeds until just combined.

Divide the batter between the paper baking cups, but only filling them half-full. Place a heaped teaspoonful of lemon curd onto each cupcake and then fill to the rim with the remaining batter. Bake for about 25–30 minutes, or until a skewer inserted into the side of a cupcake comes out clean. Leave to cool in the pans for 5 minutes then transfer to a wire rack and allow to cool completely before frosting.

To make the White Chocolate Frosting: cream together the butter, cream cheese, and confectioner's sugar, then add the melted white chocolate. Either spread the frosting using a small metal spatula or pipe the frosting onto the cooled cupcakes. Scatter with white chocolate curls and leave to set.

This could almost be a breakfast cupcake! When I can get hold of it, I make mine with blood orange marmalade. And if you happen to have it, a homemade marmalade makes these cupcakes even more divine.

ORANGE MARMALADE CUPCAKES

MAKES 12 CUPCAKES

1¼ sticks unsalted butter, softened
½ cup golden superfine sugar
2 eggs
finely grated zest of 2 oranges and 2 tbsp juice
3 tbsp Seville orange marmalade, plus extra to decorate
1 tsp vanilla extract
2 cups self-rising flour

FOR THE FROSTING

1 quantity Vanilla Buttercream Frosting (see page 88)
finely grated zest of 1 orange

Preheat the oven to 400°F, and line a cupcake pan with paper baking cups.

In a large bowl, cream together the butter and sugar. Stir in the eggs one at a time. Mix in the orange zest and juice, the marmalade, and the vanilla extract. Sift the flour into the mixture and combine until smooth.

Divide the batter between the paper baking cups and bake for about 20–25 minutes, or until a skewer inserted into the center of a cupcake comes out clean. Leave to cool in the pan for 5 minutes and then transfer to a wire rack and allow to cool completely before frosting.

Decorate the cupcakes with Vanilla Buttercream Frosting mixed with the orange zest. Finish by placing a teaspoon of marmalade on top.

This is a nice recipe to bake in the fall. It's also perfect for Halloween celebrations.

ORANGE & PUMPKIN CUPCAKES

MAKES 12 CUPCAKES

2½ cups all-purpose flour
1 tbsp baking powder
½ tsp baking soda
½ tsp ground ginger
¾ tsp ground cinnamon
½ tsp ground nutmeg
grated zest of 1 orange
7 tbsp unsalted butter, softened
1 cup superfine sugar
2 eggs
1 cup canned pumpkin
generous ⅔ cup milk

FOR THE MASCARPONE FROSTING

1⅓ cups mascarpone cheese
¾ cup confectioner's sugar, sifted
grated zest of 1 orange and
    1 tbsp juice

Preheat the oven to 400°F, and line a cupcake pan with paper baking cups.

In a large bowl, sift together the flour, baking powder, baking soda, ginger, cinnamon, and nutmeg. Then stir in the grated orange zest.

In another bowl, cream together the butter and sugar until light and fluffy. Then beat in the eggs, one at a time. Blend the canned pumpkin into this mixture and then stir in the sifted dry ingredients, a little at a time, alternating with some of the milk, blending after each addition until smooth.

Divide the batter between the paper baking cups and bake for 25 minutes, or until a skewer inserted into the center of a cupcake comes out clean. Leave to cool in the pan for 5 minutes then transfer to a wire rack and allow to cool completely before frosting.

To make the Mascarpone Frosting: beat the mascarpone cheese until light and smooth, and then gradually add the confectioner's sugar, stirring after each addition. Stir in the grated orange zest and juice, and mix until smooth. Using a small metal spatula, spread the frosting onto the top of each cupcake.

The classic lemon meringue pie turned into a delicious cupcake. You could serve these as a dessert and add a few berries for an extra finishing touch. Lemon curd is available by mail order online and in gourmet markets and some supermarkets.

LEMON MERINGUE CUPCAKES

MAKES 12 CUPCAKES

7 tbsp unsalted butter, softened
½ cup superfine sugar
seeds from 1 vanilla bean
2 eggs
¾ cup self-rising flour, sifted
finely grated zest of 1 lemon, plus
    a few strips to decorate
¼ cup lemon curd

FOR THE MERINGUE
2 egg whites
½ cup superfine sugar

Preheat the oven to 400°F, and line a cupcake pan with paper baking cups.

In a large mixing bowl, ideally using an electric hand mixer, cream together the butter, sugar, and vanilla seeds until the mixture is pale, fluffy, and well combined. Crack in the eggs one at a time, and beat them in until both are fully incorporated into the mixture. Fold in the sifted flour and the lemon zest until well combined.

Divide the batter between the paper baking cups and add a teaspoonful of lemon curd to the top of each cupcake. Bake for 15–20 minutes, or until they are pale golden brown and spring back when pressed lightly in the center.

While the cupcakes are baking, make the meringue: whisk the egg whites until they form soft peaks. Gradually add the sugar, whisking continuously, until stiff peaks form again. The mixture should be thick and glossy.

When the cakes have cooked, remove them from the oven to cool. Turn the oven off and preheat the broiler to its highest setting.

Spoon the meringue into a pastry bag fitted with a small tip and pipe it on top of each cupcake. To create a spiked effect, pipe small dots in a circle around the rim, pushing the bag down and up sharply to make a point, then repeat in a spiral until you reach the center.

Place the cupcakes under the hot broiler for 2 minutes to color the meringue (or you can use a kitchen torch).

The great British tradition of strawberries and cream in a sassy little cupcake. These are perfect for an al fresco lunch or picnic.

STRAWBERRY & CREAM CUPCAKES

MAKES 12 CUPCAKES

1½ sticks unsalted butter, softened
heaped ¾ cup superfine sugar
3 eggs, beaten
1 tsp vanilla extract
1⅓ cups self-rising flour, sifted

FOR THE FROSTING
1¼ cups strawberries, plus 6 extra,
    sliced in half, to decorate
1¼ cups regular cream cheese
2¼ cups confectioner's sugar, sifted

Preheat the oven to 400°F, and line a cupcake pan with paper baking cups.

Cream the butter and sugar together until light and fluffy, then gradually beat in the eggs. When the eggs have been incorporated add the vanilla extract and fold in the flour.

Divide the batter between the paper baking cups and bake for about 20 minutes, or until the cupcakes have risen and are golden. Leave to cool in the pan for 5 minutes then transfer to a wire rack and allow to cool completely before frosting.

To make the frosting: blend or mash the strawberries to a puree, then push them through a fine sieve to remove the seeds. Beat the cream cheese, confectioner's sugar, and strawberry puree together to form a smooth, shiny frosting. Transfer to a pastry bag and pipe the frosting onto the cooled cupcakes (see page 98 for piping tips), then place half a strawberry on top of each cupcake.

We sell lots of these delicious blueberry compote "Kiss cakes" at Cox Cookies & Cake. I like to add the berries in the center to enhance the flavor and provide a nice surprise when cutting or biting into the cupcake. In the shop we decorate them with chocolate lips painted with red edible coloring, but you can put whatever you like on top of yours.

BLUEBERRY COMPOTE CUPCAKES

MAKES 12 CUPCAKES

2 eggs
1 cup superfine sugar
½ cup sunflower oil
¼ tsp vanilla extract
2 cups all-purpose flour
pinch of salt
½ tsp baking powder
1 cup sour cream
1 quantity Vanilla Buttercream
   Frosting (see page 88)

FOR THE BLUEBERRY COMPOTE

1 cup blueberries
¼ cup superfine sugar

First make the Blueberry Compote: place the blueberries and the sugar in a small saucepan over low heat. Cook them gently, stirring constantly to prevent the sugar from catching. When the fruit starts to pop, remove the pan from the heat and set it aside to cool. If your compote has produced a lot of liquid, strain a little into a bowl to avoid adding too much extra liquid to your cupcake batter. (Any spare juice will come in handy later!)

Preheat the oven to 400°F, and line a cupcake pan with paper baking cups.

In a large bowl, beat the eggs, gradually adding the sugar while beating. Continue beating and slowly pour in the oil. Stir in the vanilla extract. In a separate bowl sift together the flour, salt, and baking powder. Stir these dry ingredients into the egg mixture in small amounts alternating with the sour cream.

Divide the batter between the paper baking cups, but fill them only half full. Then spoon 1½ teaspoons of the compote to each baking cup. Add another spoonful of batter to cover the compote, filling almost to the top of the baking cups.

Bake for 25 minutes, or until a skewer inserted into the side of a cupcake comes out clean. Leave to cool in the pans for 5 minutes then transfer to a wire rack and allow them to cool completely before frosting.

Pipe Vanilla Buttercream Frosting in spirals on top of each cupcake. If you have any excess compote or blueberry juice left over you can drizzle this on top of the frosting before adding a decoration, if using.

For this recipe you must get the beautiful stalks of red/pink "champagne" rhubarb usually in season at the beginning of the year. As well as being less fibrous, this gives a lovely color to these cute cupcakes.

It is best to make the baked rhubarb strips the day before: preheat the oven to 250°F. With a very sharp knife, cut the rhubarb sticks into 4-inch pieces and then slice each piece very thinly lengthwise. Line a cookie sheet with parchment paper or a silicone baking mat. Arrange the rhubarb strips on the prepared cookie sheet, dust them generously with confectioner's sugar, and bake for 2–3 hours, or until dried out and crisp. Do not overcook them or you will lose the beautiful pink color.

Preheat the oven to 400°F, and line a cupcake pan with paper baking cups.

Cream the butter and sugar until pale and fluffy. Add the eggs, then slowly pour in the milk. Sift in the flour and ginger. Divide the batter between the baking cups. Bake for 18–20 minutes, or until a skewer inserted into the center of a cupcake comes out clean. Leave to cool in the pan for 5 minutes then transfer to a wire rack and allow to cool completely.

To make the Rhubarb Compote: place all the ingredients in a small pan and heat gently to boiling point (you want the rhubarb to just release its natural juices and turn a beautiful shade of pink). Leave to bubble and reduce for 2–3 minutes. Once the rhubarb has softened and the liquid has turned syrupy, remove the pan from the heat and leave to cool completely.

Use a cutter ¾ inches in width to cut ⅓ inch deep into the center of each cupcake to make a space for the compote. Spoon the compote into these spaces and then pipe vanilla frosting onto the top. Once the frosting has set, arrange the dried pieces of baked rhubarb decoratively on top of each cupcake.

RHUBARB CUPCAKES

MAKES 12 CUPCAKES

2¼ sticks unsalted butter, softened
1 cup soft brown sugar
3 eggs
1¾ cups self-rising flour
2 tsp ground ginger
¾ cup milk
1 quantity Vanilla Buttercream
    Frosting (see page 88)

FOR THE BAKED RHUBARB STRIPS

2 sticks of pink rhubarb
confectioner's sugar, for dusting

FOR THE RHUBARB COMPOTE

1 cup trimmed and finely diced
    rhubarb
2 tbsp superfine sugar
1 tsp ground ginger
1 tbsp water

With their crumbly topping, these are more of a dessert than a cupcake—you could even serve them hot with runny custard, cream, or ice cream.

APPLE CRISP CUPCAKES

MAKES 12 CUPCAKES

2 all-purpose apples, peeled, cored, and diced
1 tsp ground cinnamon
½ tsp baking soda
7 tbsp butter, softened
1 heaped cup soft brown sugar
2 eggs
2¾ cups self-rising flour
confectioner's sugar, for dusting

FOR THE CRISP TOPPING
scant ½ cup all-purpose flour
⅓ cup soft brown sugar
½ tsp ground cinnamon
⅓ cup cold unsalted butter

Preheat the oven to 400°F, and line a cupcake pan with paper baking cups.

First make the crisp; add the flour, sugar, and cinnamon to a bowl. Cut the unsalted butter into the flour mixture until it resembles coarse crumbs. Set the crisp aside.

Put the apples in a saucepan with the cinnamon and cook over very low heat until mushy. Leave to cool, then drain through a fine sieve to remove any liquid. Then measure out 1 cup of the drained apple, place it in a bowl, and stir in the baking soda. Set aside.

In a large bowl, cream the butter and sugar together, and then beat in the eggs. Fold the self-rising flour and the apples alternately into the butter and sugar mixture and combine.

Divide the batter between the paper baking cups. Divide the crisp mixture evenly among the tops and bake for 20–25 minutes, or until golden brown on top and a skewer inserted into the center of a cupcake comes out clean.

Leave to cool in the pan for 5 minutes then transfer to a wire rack and allow to cool completely. When cool, finish with a dusting of confectioner's sugar.

MAURITIUS PINEAPPLE CUPCAKES

This recipe is inspired by a fabulous dessert of spit-roasted baby pineapple with Amaretto that I once had in Mauritius. All the luscious flavors are here in these cupcakes.

MAKES 12 CUPCAKES

1⅓ cups all-purpose flour
⅓ cup ground almonds
1 tsp baking powder
1⅛ sticks unsalted butter, softened
1½ cups golden superfine sugar
3 eggs at room temperature
1 tsp pure vanilla extract
½ tsp pure almond extract
½ cup milk
⅓ cup Amaretto
1⅔ cups heavy cream

FOR THE FLAMBÉED PINEAPPLE
½ cup superfine sugar
1 small pineapple, peeled, cored, and finely diced
scant ½ cup Amaretto
scant ½ cup heavy cream
1 tbsp fresh orange juice
seeds from 1 vanilla bean

Preheat the oven to 400°F, and line a cupcake pan with paper baking cups.

In a bowl, sift together the flour, ground almonds, and baking powder. In another large bowl, cream the butter and sugar until pale and fluffy. Add the eggs, one at a time, beating each one until incorporated. Stir in the vanilla and almond extracts. Add the flour mixture in three batches, alternating with the milk in two additions, and mixing until just combined. If using an electric hand mixer, reduce the speed to low.

Divide the batter between the paper baking cups, to fill each three-quarters full. Bake for 18–20 minutes, or until a skewer inserted into the center of a cupcake comes out clean. Set the pan on a wire rack. Immediately prick holes into the tops of the cupcakes with a toothpick then pour a teaspoon of Amaretto over each one. Leave to cool completely before removing from the pan.

To make the Flambéed Pineapple: in a large pan, heat the sugar over medium heat, stirring, until the sugar dissolves and turns golden brown. Add the diced pineapple and gently toss it in the dissolved sugar. Carefully pour in the Amaretto and ignite the alcohol. If there is a lot of liquid still in the pan once the flames subside and the caramel melts, strain a little away. Then stir in the cream, orange juice, and vanilla seeds. Bring to a boil, stirring occasionally until thickened, for about 5 minutes. Remove from the heat and allow to cool completely. When ready to serve, whip the cream to soft peaks and spread it on top of each cooled cupcake. Place a generous spoonful of Flambéed Pineapple on top of each one.

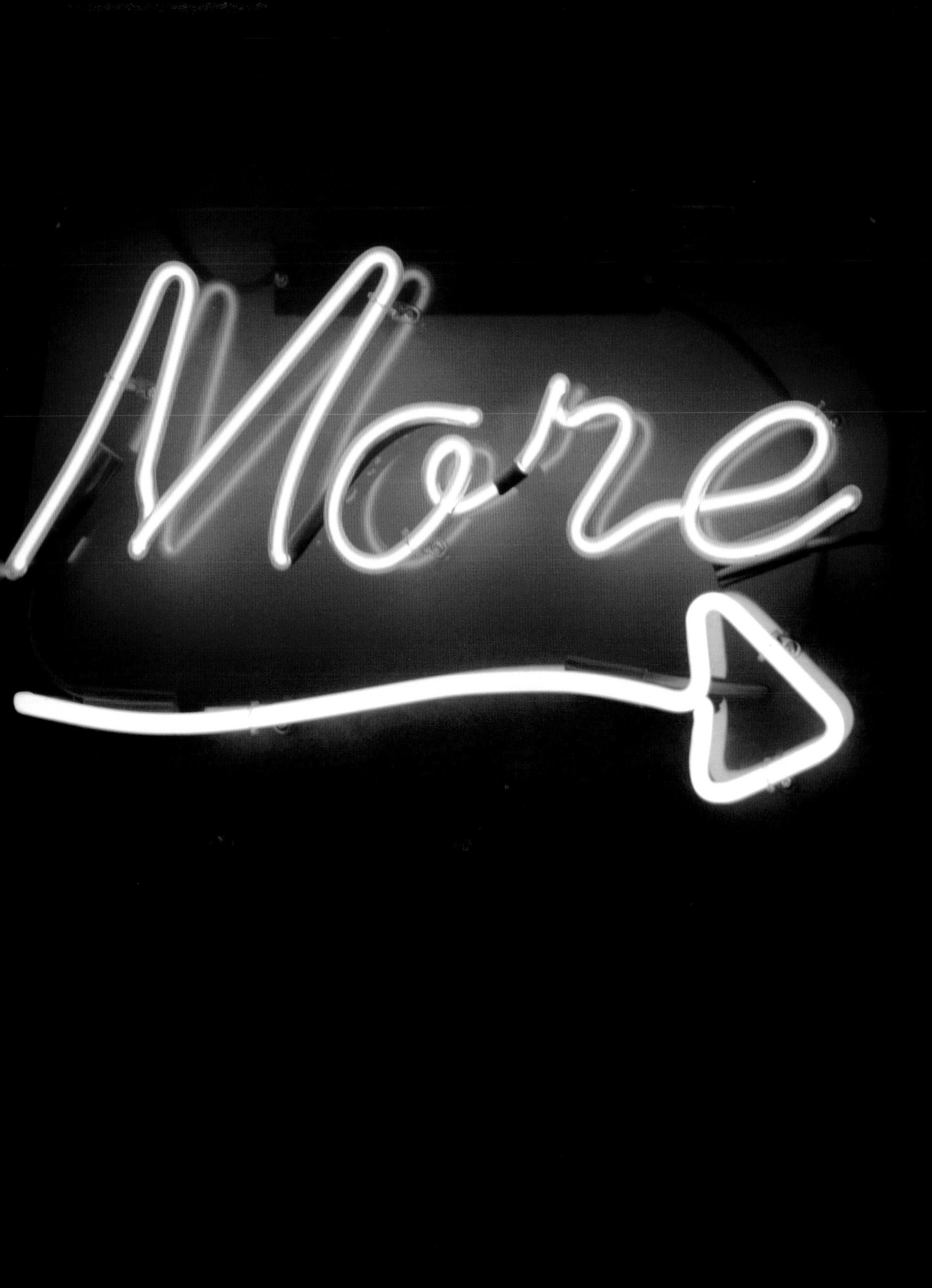
More

3

The rich chocolate and all the lovely exotic spices in these cakes work very well together, and just when you thought you'd tasted everything, a lovely hot sensation hits you as the cayenne chile-flavored frosting works its wonders…another one for adults only!

MEXICAN CHOCOLATE CUPCAKES

MAKES 12 CUPCAKES

1⅓ cups all-purpose flour
1 heaped cup superfine sugar
¼ cup unsweetened cocoa powder
1 tsp baking soda
1 tsp cinnamon
¼ tsp ground nutmeg
1 tsp vanilla extract
1 tbsp white wine vinegar
¼ cup + 1 tbsp sunflower oil
chile pepper cake decorations,
    to decorate

FOR THE FROSTING

3½oz semisweet chocolate,
    broken into pieces
1⅜ sticks unsalted butter
1¼ cups confectioner's sugar
¼ tsp ground cayenne pepper

Preheat the oven to 400°F, and line a cupcake pan with paper baking cups.

Sift together the flour, sugar, cocoa powder, baking soda, cinnamon, and nutmeg into a bowl. In a large bowl, blend together the vanilla extract, vinegar, oil, and 1 cup cold water. Mix the dry ingredients into this mixture until well combined and the batter is smooth—a stand mixer or an electric hand mixer will help in doing this.

Divide the batter between the paper baking cups (it will be fairly liquid, so you may want to use a large measuring jug to pour it). Bake for 20–25 minutes, or until a skewer inserted into the center of a cupcake comes out clean. Allow the cupcakes to cool in the pan for 5 minutes, and then transfer them to a wire rack to cool completely.

To make the frosting: melt the chocolate in a heatproof bowl set over a saucepan of barely simmering water, making sure the bowl does not touch the surface of the water. When melted leave to cool.

Whisk the butter and confectioner's sugar together until pale and fluffy, then whisk in the cooled melted chocolate and the cayenne pepper. Pipe the frosting onto the cooled cupcakes. Set a chile pepper cake decoration on top to finish.

This is my favorite Italian dessert in a cupcake. The light coffee-flavored cupcake covered with a mascarpone and Marsala frosting makes a truly delicious combination. These cupcakes must be eaten on the day they are made.

TIRAMISU CUPCAKES

MAKES 12 CUPCAKES

3½ tbsp unsalted butter
2/3 cup golden superfine sugar
4 eggs
1 cup all-purpose flour
1 level tbsp instant espresso
   granules dissolved in
   2 tsp boiling water

FOR THE FROSTING
1 cup + 2 tbsp mascarpone cheese
1¼ cups golden confectioner's
   sugar sifted
1 tbsp Marsala wine
unsweetened cocoa powder, to
   decorate
confectioner's sugar, to decorate

Preheat the oven to 400°F, and line a cupcake pan with paper baking cups.

Put the butter in a heatproof bowl and melt in the microwave or in a heatproof bowl placed over a saucepan of barely simmering water, making sure the bowl does not touch the surface of the water.

Put the sugar and eggs in another bowl and, ideally using a stand mixer or an electric hand mixer, cream them together until light and frothy and doubled in volume—this will take several minutes.

Sift the flour and gently fold half of it into the mixture. Mix the coffee into the melted butter and pour half of this into the mixture. Add the remaining flour, followed by the rest of the coffee and butter mixture. Work gently as you fold these in.

Divide the batter between the paper baking cups and bake for 25 minutes, or until a skewer inserted into the center of a cupcake comes out clean. Leave to cool in the pan for 5 minutes and then set the individual cupcakes out on a wire rack and allow to cool completely.

To make the frosting: beat the mascarpone cheese with the golden confectioner's sugar, then add the Marsala and combine. Spread this on top of each cupcake and finish with a generous dusting of unsweetened cocoa powder and confectioner's sugar.

Dark chocolate and coffee always make a good combination, so I've put these two fabulous flavors together to create the most delicious cupcakes.

MOCHA CUPCAKES

MAKES 12 CUPCAKES

1½ sticks unsalted butter, softened
heaped ¾ cup superfine sugar
3 eggs
1 tbsp hot water mixed with 1 tsp instant coffee
1¼ cups all-purpose flour
¼ cup unsweetened cocoa powder

FOR THE FROSTING

7 tbsp unsalted butter, softened
1¼ cups confectioner's sugar
2 tsp fresh coffee, ideally espresso, cooled
2oz melted semisweet chocolate
chocolate coffee beans, to decorate
edible gold paint, to decorate
  (optional, see page 159 for suppliers)

Preheat the oven to 400°F, and line a cupcake pan with paper baking cups.

Cream the butter and sugar together until light and fluffy, then add the eggs one at the time, beating well after each addition until combined and the mixture is smooth. Stir in the coffee mixture. Sift the flour and unsweenetend cocoa powder onto the mixture and fold it in.

Divide the batter between the paper baking cups and bake for 20 minutes, or until a skewer inserted into the center of a cupcake comes out clean. Leave to cool in the pan for 5 minutes and then set the individual cupcakes out on a wire rack and allow to cool completely.

To make the frosting: beat the butter and confectioner's sugar together until pale and fluffy. Add the coffee and melted chocolate, and beat until smooth. Pipe or spoon this onto each cupcake and, if using, finish by decorating them with some chocolate coffee beans lightly painted with edible gold paint.

This powerful recipe will give an afternoon tea party a punchy start! The addition of the ginger in syrup makes this little wonder very moist and extremely difficult to resist.

PRESERVED GINGER CUPCAKES

MAKES 18 CUPCAKES

2¼ sticks unsalted butter
1⅓ cups dark brown soft sugar
1⅓ cups molasses
1¼ cups milk
3 eggs, lightly beaten
1 cup ginger in syrup, drained and
    diced, plus extra to decorate
3¼ cups all-purpose flour
2 tsp baking powder
1 tsp mixed spice
2 tsp ground ginger
1½ quantities Vanilla Buttercream
    Frosting (see page 88)

Preheat the oven to 400°F, and line a 12-hole and a 6-hole cupcake or muffin pan with paper baking cups.

Put the butter, sugar, and molasses in a saucepan and heat gently for about 5 minutes until the butter and sugar have melted. Stir in the milk and leave to cool before beating in the eggs.

Mix the diced ginger and remaining ingredients together in a large bowl. Pour in the melted mixture and, using a wooden spoon, mix it all together to form a smooth thick batter.

Divide the batter between the paper baking cups and bake for about 25 minutes, or until a skewer inserted into the center of a cupcake comes out clean. Leave to cool in the pans for 5 minutes then transfer to a wire rack. Allow the cupcakes to cool completely before frosting them.

I like to finish mine with Vanilla Buttercream Frosting, and with some more diced ginger scattered on the top.

This light and fruity cupcake has just the right balance of the tea flavor. The delicate Italian candied fruits have been soaked in orange liqueur and look like jewels on top, adding a dash of glamor.

LADY GREY CUPCAKES

MAKES 12 CUPCAKES

²/₃ cup mixed candied fruit, finely diced, plus extra to decorate
2–3 tbsp orange liqueur
2 Lady Grey tea bags
1 scant cup water
2 eggs
1 cup golden superfine sugar
½ cup vegetable oil
1 tsp vanilla extract
2 cups all-purpose flour
½ tsp baking powder

FOR THE TOPPING

1 quantity Cream Cheese Frosting (see page 89)
edible gold leaf (see page 159 for suppliers)

The day before you want to bake, mix together the chopped candied fruits and the orange liqueur in a small bowl. Leave it to soak overnight.

Place the tea bags in another small bowl. Bring the water to a boil and pour it onto the tea bags. Leave to infuse to create a strong tea then discard the tea bags and allow the tea to cool.

Preheat the oven to 400°F, and line a cupcake pan with paper baking cups.

In a large bowl, beat the eggs and gradually add the sugar while still beating. Continue beating while slowly pouring in the oil. Stir in the vanilla extract. Sift the flour and baking powder together. Fold these into the mixture a little at a time, alternating with additions of some of the strong tea, until the batter is smooth.

Strain the candied fruits, reserving the orange liqueur. Fold the fruits into the cupcake batter and then divide the batter between the baking cups. Bake for 20 minutes, or until a skewer inserted into the center of a cupcake comes out clean. Once the cupcakes have cooked but while they are still warm, prick several holes into the top of each cupcake using a toothpick. Spoon the reserved orange liqueur onto the cupcakes then leave them to cool in the pan before decorating.

Pipe Cream Cheese Frosting on top of each cupcake and decorate with flecks of edible gold leaf to finish.

If you enjoy the rich flavor of licorice, this recipe is for you. I like using this batter as my base for Halloween cakes because of the natural dark color of the cupcake and the frosting.

LICORICE CUPCAKES

MAKES 16 CUPCAKES

3½oz black licorice laces
¾ cup milk
2¼ sticks unsalted butter, softened
¼ cup Barbados sugar
4 eggs
1½ cups self-rising flour
½ cup all-purpose flour

FOR THE LICORICE FROSTING

3½oz black licorice laces, plus
    some extra laces to decorate
scant ½ cup confectioner's sugar
3½ tbsp unsalted butter, softened

Preheat the oven to 400°F, and line a 12-hole and a 4-hole cupcake or muffin pan with paper baking cups.

Place the licorice laces and the milk in a saucepan over low heat. Stir until the licorice has dissolved. Set aside to cool.

Place the butter and sugar in a bowl and cream together until pale and creamy. Add the eggs one at a time, beating well after each addition until well combined and smooth. Sift the flours together and fold them into the mixture together with the cooled licorice milk. Stir until smooth.

Divide the batter between the paper baking cups to fill them three-quarters full. Bake for 20 minutes, or until a skewer inserted into the center of a cupcake comes out clean. Leave to cool in the pans for 5 minutes then transfer to a wire rack and allow to cool completely before frosting.

To make the Licorice Frosting: add the licorice laces to a heatproof bowl and place over a saucepan of barely simmering water, making sure the bowl does not touch the surface of the water. Heat until completely dissolved, stirring occasionally. Remove from the heat and allow to cool.

Beat the confectioner's sugar and butter together until pale and smooth. Still mixing, add in the dissolved licorice and beat until smooth.

Pipe or spoon the frosting on top of the cooled cupcakes and decorate with black licorice laces.

This is a classic cupcake that could be a reliable base for any topping—and we all have a day when a good simple vanilla cupcake does the trick!

MADAGASCAN VANILLA CUPCAKES

MAKES 12 CUPCAKES

2¼ sticks unsalted butter, softened
1¼ cups superfine sugar
4 eggs
1 tsp vanilla extract, preferably
    Madagascan
1½ cups self-rising flour
½ cup all-purpose flour
¾ cup milk
1 quantity Vanilla Buttercream
    Frosting (see page 88) or Cream
    Cheese Frosting (see page 89)
sugar cake decorations, to decorate

Preheat the oven to 400°F, and line a cupcake pan with paper baking cups.

Place the butter and sugar in a bowl and cream together until pale and creamy. Add the eggs, one at a time, then add the vanilla extract and beat until well combined. Sift the flours together then fold them in, a little at a time, alternating with some of the milk. Stir until smooth.

Divide the mixture between the paper baking cups and bake for 20 minutes, or until a skewer inserted into the center of a cupcake comes out clean. Leave to cool in the pan for 5 minutes, then transfer to a wire rack and allow to cool completely before frosting.

Pipe Vanilla Buttercream Frosting or Cream Cheese Frosting on top, and scatter with sugar decorations to finish.

One of the most popular flavors in Brittany, where I come from in France, is salted butter caramel. I grew up eating ice cream, candies, and spreads flavored by this now very fashionable combination. These cupcakes are so decadent with a rich caramel sauce poured over the top.

SALTED BUTTER CARAMEL CUPCAKES

MAKES 12 CUPCAKES

1⅓ cups self-rising flour

1 tsp baking soda

5 tbsp unsalted butter, softened

½ heaped cup Barbados sugar

2 eggs, lightly beaten

1 tsp vanilla extract

2 tbsp milk

2oz toffee or pieces of fudge, cut into small dice

FOR THE CARAMEL SAUCE

⅔ cup superfine sugar

5 tbsp salted butter

¼ cup + 1 tbsp heavy cream

1 tsp vanilla extract

FOR THE BUTTERCREAM FROSTING

1⅜ sticks unsalted butter, softened

1¼ cups confectioner's sugar

1 tsp vanilla extract

1 tsp caramel extract (optional)

few flakes of sea salt, to decorate

Preheat the oven to 400°F, and line a cupcake pan with paper baking cups.

Sift the flour and baking soda together into a bowl and set aside. Using a stand mixer or an electric hand mixer, cream the butter and sugar together for a good 5 minutes until very light and fluffy. Add the beaten eggs gradually, beating between each addition and adding 1 tablespoon of flour about halfway through to stop the mixture from curdling. Beat in the vanilla extract then fold in the remaining flour, the milk, and the toffee or fudge.

Divide the batter between the paper baking cups and bake for 15–20 minutes, or until the tops spring back when pressed with a finger. Leave to cool in the pan for 5 minutes, then transfer to a wire rack and allow to cool completely.

To make the Caramel Sauce; dissolve the sugar in ¼ cup water in a small heavy saucepan over very low heat. Increase the heat and simmer. As soon as you have a nice blond-colored caramel remove the pan from the heat. Add the butter—be careful because it may splutter. Continue stirring as you add the cream and vanilla extract. Stir until smooth then leave to cool.

To make the Buttercream Frosting; cream the butter and confectioner's sugar together for at least 5 minutes then beat in the vanilla and caramel extracts.

Use a small metal spatula to spread Buttercream Frosting onto the cupcakes. Pour a little Caramel Sauce over the top, and scatter each cupcake with a few sea salt flakes to finish.

Since traveling more often to the Far East, I have really begun to appreciate the taste of Asian food. The fusion of sweet and sour flavors works so well in traditional Asian cooking, and in these delicious cupcakes, too.

FUSION CUPCAKES

MAKES 12 CUPCAKES

2-inch piece of fresh ginger root, peeled
2 lemon grass stalks, trimmed and roughly chopped
2 tsp vanilla extract
7 tbsp butter, softened
heaped ¾ cup golden superfine sugar
2 eggs
1½ cups + 1 tbsp self-rising flour
½ cup milk

FOR THE FROSTING

7 tbsp butter, softened
3 cups confectioner's sugar
3 tbsp milk
1 tsp vanilla extract
3½oz mixed exotic dried fruits (such as mango, coconut, or pineapple), to decorate

Preheat the oven to 400°F, and line a cupcake pan with paper baking cups.

Place the ginger, lemon grass, and vanilla extract in a food processor and process to a fine paste. Push the paste through a sieve to extract the juice. Discard the pulp.

Cream the butter and sugar together until light and fluffy. Add the reserved juice, then add the eggs one at a time, beating slowly until just combined. Add the flour and milk in alternate batches. Stir with a wooden spoon until just combined.

Divide the batter between the paper baking cups and bake for 15–20 minutes, or until a skewer inserted into the center of a cupcake comes out clean. Leave to cool in the pan for 5 minutes, then transfer the individual cupcakes to a wire rack and allow to cool completely before frosting.

To make the frosting; beat the butter until very pale, then gradually beat in the confectioner's sugar. Add the milk and vanilla extract and beat until well combined.

Use a small metal spatula or pastry bag to decorate the cakes with the frosting. Roughly chop the dried exotic fruit and arrange it on top as decoration.

One of my favorite things about the arrival of "gastropubs" in Britain is the rebirth of traditional English desserts, like Sticky Toffee Pudding. When properly made, traditional English desserts are rich, filling, and so indulgent. To make these cupcakes cute and tiny, bake them in smaller standard cupcake cups and not the larger "muffin" type. Bake for 12 minutes then check to see if they are done.

STICKY TOFFEE CUPCAKES

MAKES 12 STANDARD CUPCAKES

2/3 cup hot water

1 tea bag

3 tbsp dried apricots, roughly chopped

heaped 1/4 cup dates, pitted and roughly chopped

1 1/4 cups self-rising flour

1 tsp baking powder

1/4 cup Barbados sugar

1 tbsp light corn syrup

2 large eggs, lightly beaten

3 1/2 tbsp butter, melted

FOR THE TOFFEE SAUCE

1/4 cup superfine sugar

3 1/2 tbsp butter

scant 1/2 cup heavy cream

light cream, to serve

Preheat the oven to 400°F, and line a cupcake pan with paper baking cups.

Put the hot water, tea bag, apricots, and dates in a saucepan, bring to a boil, then remove from the heat and leave to soak and cool.

Sift the flour and baking powder together into a large mixing bowl. Drain the fruits, then add them to the flour with the Barbados sugar, light corn syrup, eggs, and butter. Mix together until blended.

Divide the batter between the paper baking cups and bake for 25–30 minutes, or until a skewer inserted into the center of a cupcake comes out clean.

Toward the end of the baking time, make the toffee sauce: heat the superfine sugar in a heavy saucepan until you get a dark caramel. Add the butter, stirring well with a wooden spoon. Deglaze the pan by stirring in the heavy cream. When all the caramel has dissolved, pour it through a sieve into a warmed measuring jug.

When the cupcakes are done, carefully remove the paper baking cups and serve immediately, piping hot, with the toffee sauce and lots of light cream.

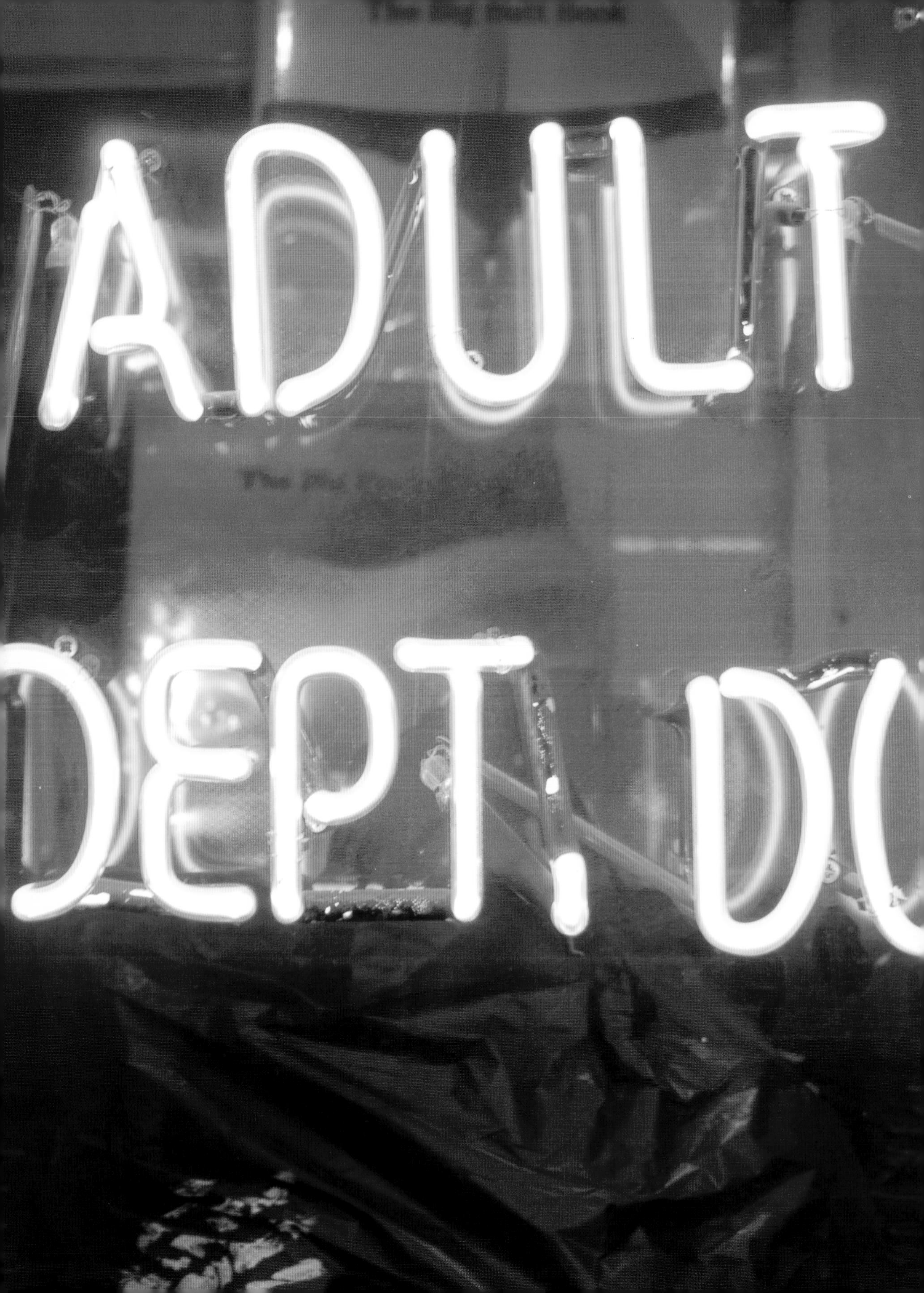
ADULT
DEPT.

4

This fat-free cupcake is very light and delicate, like an angel, while the raspberry frosting adds a great fruity touch. These cupcakes are absolutely perfect for summer.

ANGEL FOOD CUPCAKES WITH RASPBERRY FROSTING

MAKES 12 CUPCAKES

1 cup less 1 heaped tbsp
    all-purpose flour
¾ cup confectioner's sugar
1 tsp cream of tartar
8 egg whites
pinch of salt
¾ cup superfine sugar
½ tsp vanilla extract
½ tsp almond extract

FOR THE RASPBERRY FROSTING

heaped ¾ cup fresh raspberries,
    plus extra to decorate
1⅛ sticks unsalted butter, softened
    slightly and diced
2¼ cups confectioner's sugar,
    sifted, plus more to decorate
    (optional)

Preheat the oven to 400°F, and line a cupcake pan with paper baking cups.

Sift the flour, confectioner's sugar, and cream of tartar into a bowl and set aside. In a large bowl whisk the egg whites until frothy, ideally using a stand mixer or an electric hand mixer. Then add the salt and gradually begin to add the superfine sugar a tablespoonful at a time. Continue whisking until stiff peaks form—this will take several minutes.

Stir in the vanilla and almond extracts, then add the flour and confectioner's sugar. Fold gently with a large metal spoon until combined. Be quick—if the mixture is left to stand, it will collapse and spoil the light consistency of the cakes.

Divide the batter between the paper baking cups and bake for 15–20 minutes, or until a skewer inserted into the center of a cupcake comes out clean. Leave to cool in the pan for 5 minutes, then transfer to a wire rack and allow to cool completely. These cakes will sink a little as they cool.

To make the Raspberry Frosting; rub the raspberries through a fine sieve to yield about 2 tablespoons of raspberry puree and set aside. Add the butter to a clean bowl and cream until soft. Sift in some of the confectioner's sugar, then beat it in to combine. Repeat this process until all of the sugar has been incorporated into the butter. Beat in the raspberry puree until the frosting has a spreading consistency.

Using a pastry bag fitted with a pastry tip, pipe the frosting (see page 98 for piping hints), and decorate with fresh raspberries. Dust with confectioner's sugar to finish, if using.

I think that if I was on a diet, I would miss chocolate the most. But don't worry, you can spoil yourself with this recipe…but not too often!

LOW-FAT CHOCOLATE CUPCAKES

MAKES 12 CUPCAKES

¾ cup all-purpose flour
¼ cup unsweetened cocoa powder
4 large eggs
⅔ cup superfine sugar
2 tbsp chocolate chips

FOR THE TOPPING
heaped ¼ cup low-fat spread
⅔ cup low-fat cream cheese
3½oz unsweetened chocolate,
    melted and cooled
artificial sweetener, to taste

Preheat the oven to 400°F, and line a cupcake pan with paper baking cups.

Sift together the flour and unsweetened cocoa powder. In a large bowl, whisk together the eggs and sugar using an electric hand mixer until the mixture becomes thick and foamy and has doubled in size. This may take up to 10 minutes, but it is worth the effort because the more air that gets in the lighter the sponge will be. Gently fold in the flour and cocoa powder followed by the chocolate chips, being careful to knock out as little air as possible.

Divide the batter between the baking cups and bake for 20 minutes, or until a skewer inserted into the center of a cupcake comes out clean. Leave to cool in the pan for 5 minutes, then transfer the individual cupcakes to a wire rack and allow them to cool completely.

To make the topping: beat the low-fat spread with the cream cheese, then stir in the cooled melted chocolate. Sweeten the frosting to taste with the artificial sweetener, then frost the cupcakes.

As much as I always try not to compromise on ingredients, it is still possible to indulge yourself even if you are following a low-fat diet. Despite being low in fat, these cupcakes are delicious, light, and tasty. They won't make you feel guilty and one of these is much more enjoyable than an apple!

LOW-FAT WHITE CHOCOLATE & BERRY CUPCAKES

MAKES 12 CUPCAKES

⅓ cup + 2 tbsp low-fat spread
½ cup golden superfine sugar
1⅓ cups self-rising flour, sifted
2 eggs
½ tsp vanilla extract
¼ cup skim milk

FOR THE WHITE CHOCOLATE TOPPING

2oz white chocolate, broken
    into pieces
⅔ cup low-fat cream cheese
2 tbsp confectioner's sugar, plus
    extra to decorate
1⅓ cups mixed raspberries,
blueberries, and red currants,
    for decorating
white chocolate curls, to decorate

Preheat the oven to 400°F, and line a cupcake pan with paper baking cups.

Add all the cake ingredients to a large mixing bowl and beat for 2–3 minutes, ideally using an electric hand mixer, until pale and fluffy.

Divide the batter between the paper baking cups and bake for 18–20 minutes, or until a skewer inserted into the center of a cupcake comes out clean. Leave to cool in the pan for 5 minutes and then set the individual cupcakes on a wire rack and allow them to cool completely.

To make the White Chocolate Topping: put the white chocolate in a large heatproof bowl and place over a saucepan of barely simmering water, making sure the bowl does not touch the surface of the water. Heat until completely melted. Allow to cool slightly, then beat in the cream cheese and confectioner's sugar until smooth. Chill in the refrigerator until it firms up a little.

Using a small metal spatula or pastry bag, cover the cupcakes with the topping. Decorate with the berries, dust with confectioner's sugar, and scatter some white chocolate curls on top.

Yes, it is possible—these dainty cupcakes are fat-free and delicious, too. The crystallized flowers give them a perfect look for a chic afternoon treat.

FAT-FREE JASMINE & VIOLET CUPCAKES

MAKES 12 CUPCAKES

FOR THE CRYSTALLIZED FLOWERS
a few violet and jasmine flowers
1 egg white, lightly beaten
2 tbsp granulated sugar

3 eggs
1/3 cup golden superfine sugar
2/3 cup self-rising flour
1 tsp vanilla extract
2 drops of vanilla essence

FOR THE JASMINE DRIZZLE
1 jasmine tea bag
3 tbsp boiling water
2 cups confectioner's sugar

First make the crystallized edible flowers; to day before you want to bake, dip the violet and jasmine flowers in the beaten egg white, then set them on a sheet of waxed paper. Dust the flowers generously all over with granulated sugar and leave them to dry overnight.

Preheat the oven to 400°F, and line a cupcake pan with paper baking cups.

In a large bowl beat the eggs and sugar together using an electric hand mixer until light, fluffy, and doubled in volume. Sift the flour and gently fold it into the mixture, followed by the vanilla extract and essence.

Divide the batter between the paper baking cups and bake for 20 minutes, or until a skewer inserted into the center of a cupcake comes out clean. Leave to cool in the pan for 5 minutes, then transfer the individual cupcakes to a wire rack and allow to cool completely.

To make the Jasmine Drizzle; put the tea bag in a small heatproof bowl and pour the boiling water over it. Leave to infuse until the tea is very strong. Discard the tea bag. Mix the confectioner's sugar into the tea until you get a thick, runny consistency. Drizzle it onto the cooled cupcakes and, before the mixture sets, decorate the cupcakes with the crystallized violet and jasmine flowers.

These cupcakes are based on my favorite French pear dessert, Tarte Bordaloue. There is, of course, no pastry in this version and, being gluten-free, it is perfect for anyone with a gluten allergy.

GLUTEN-FREE PEAR & ALMOND CUPCAKES

MAKES 12 CUPCAKES

3 cups + 1 tbsp ground almonds
1 tbsp gluten-free baking powder
½ cup superfine sugar
7 tbsp butter, melted
2 eggs, beaten
1 cup milk
3 canned baby pears, drained
¼ cup sliced almonds
confectioner's sugar, to decorate

FOR THE POACHED PEARS

2 large ripe pears, peeled, cored, and quartered
½ cup superfine sugar
1 scant cup water
1 vanilla bean, split lengthwise

If time allows poach the pears the day before. Put the sugar, water, and vanilla bean in a saucepan. Slowly bring to a boil, stirring continuously until the sugar has dissolved. Add the pear quarters, cover, and simmer over low heat for 15 minutes. Remove from the heat and set aside to cool.

When you are ready to bake, preheat the oven to 400°F, and line a cupcake pan with paper baking cups.

In a large bowl, mix together the ground almonds, baking powder, and sugar. Add the melted butter, eggs, and milk, and mix until creamy. Drain the poached pears, dice them finely, then fold them into the mixture.

Divide the batter between the paper baking cups. Chop each of the canned baby pears into quarters (you should have 12 pieces) and place one baby pear quarter standing upright on top of each cupcake. Scatter with the sliced almonds and bake for 25–30 minutes, or until a skewer inserted into the center of a cupcake comes out clean. Leave to cool in the pan for 5 minutes, then transfer to a wire rack and allow to cool completely. Dust with confectioner's sugar before serving.

These energy-packed cupcakes are perfect for kids' lunchboxes or for a healthy treat or snack to help keep you going through the day.

GRANOLA & MIXED SPICE CUPCAKES

MAKES 12 CUPCAKES

1½ cups whole-wheat flour

heaped 1¼ cups granola

2 tsp baking powder

1 tsp mixed spice

1 tbsp poppy seeds

1 cup dried apricots, chopped

½ cup golden raisins

3 tbsp sunflower oil

2 eggs

¾ cup milk

⅓ cup liquid honey

Preheat the oven to 400°F, and line a cupcake pan with paper baking cups.

In a large mixing bowl, mix together the flour, a heaped ¾ cup of the granola, the baking powder, mixed spice, poppy seeds, and dried fruit.

In another bowl, whisk together the oil, eggs, milk, and honey until well blended. Pour the mixture into the dry ingredients and quickly stir.

Divide the batter between the paper baking cups and scatter the remaining ½ cup of granola evenly over the tops. Bake for 25 minutes, or until a skewer inserted into the center of a cupcake comes out clean. Leave to cool in the pan for 5 minutes, then transfer to a wire rack and allow to cool completely.

They will keep in the fridge for 2–3 days, or can be frozen.

These flour-free cupcakes are perfect for people who have a gluten allergy. The decadent addition of ground almonds makes them very moist, while the final drizzle of spicy syrup adds to their great taste.

GLUTEN-FREE PROVENÇAL ORANGE CUPCAKES

MAKES 12 CUPCAKES

1¾ cups ground almonds
¾ cup superfine sugar
2 tsp gluten-free baking powder
4 eggs, beaten
1 cup less 2 tbsp sunflower oil
finely grated zest of 1 lemon
finely grated zest of 2 oranges, ideally Seville, plus a few extra strands of zest to decorate

FOR THE SYRUP

juice of 1 lemon
juice of 2 oranges, ideally Seville
½ cup superfine sugar
pinch of ground cloves
2 tsp ground cinnamon

Preheat the oven to 400°F, and line a cupcake pan with paper baking cups.

In a mixing bowl, combine the ground almonds, superfine sugar, and baking powder. Add the eggs and oil, and mix gently together. Stir the lemon and orange zest into the mixture.

Divide the batter between the paper baking cups and bake for 30 minutes, or until a skewer inserted into the center of a cupcake comes out clean. Leave to cool in the pan for 5 minutes, then transfer the individual cupcakes to a wire rack to cool slightly.

To make the syrup: pour the lemon and orange juices into a small saucepan. Add the sugar, cloves, and cinnamon. Bring to a boil, then reduce the heat and simmer for 3 minutes.

While the cupcakes are still warm, pierce the tops several times with a toothpick. Spoon the syrup onto the cupcakes and allow it to soak in a little while they cool. Decorate with strands of orange zest to finish.

These breakfast cupcakes make a delicious, nourishing kickstart to any day. I like to eat mine straight from the oven with honey, because you get all the hearty flavor.

ZUCCHINI CUPCAKES

MAKES 12 CUPCAKES

1²/₃ cups whole-wheat flour
2 tsp baking powder
1 tsp mixed spices
²/₃ cup mixed seeds (such as pumpkin, sesame, and sunflower seeds)
2 eggs
1 cup less 2 tbsp milk
4 tsp vegetable oil
4 tsp liquid honey
5oz zucchini, trimmed and then grated
liquid honey and Greek-style yogurt, to serve (optional)

Preheat the oven to 400°F, and line a cupcake pan with paper baking cups.

In a large bowl, thoroughly mix together all the dry ingredients (but do not sift the flour—you want to keep all the goodness from the whole wheat). Stir in all of the liquid ingredients and combine until smooth. Gently fold in the grated zucchini.

Divide the batter between the paper baking cups and bake for 25 minutes or until a skewer inserted into the center of a cupcake comes out clean. Leave to cool in the pan for 5 minutes, then transfer the individual cupcakes to a wire rack and allow to cool completely.

To serve, drizzle with honey and some Greek-syle yogurt, if liked.

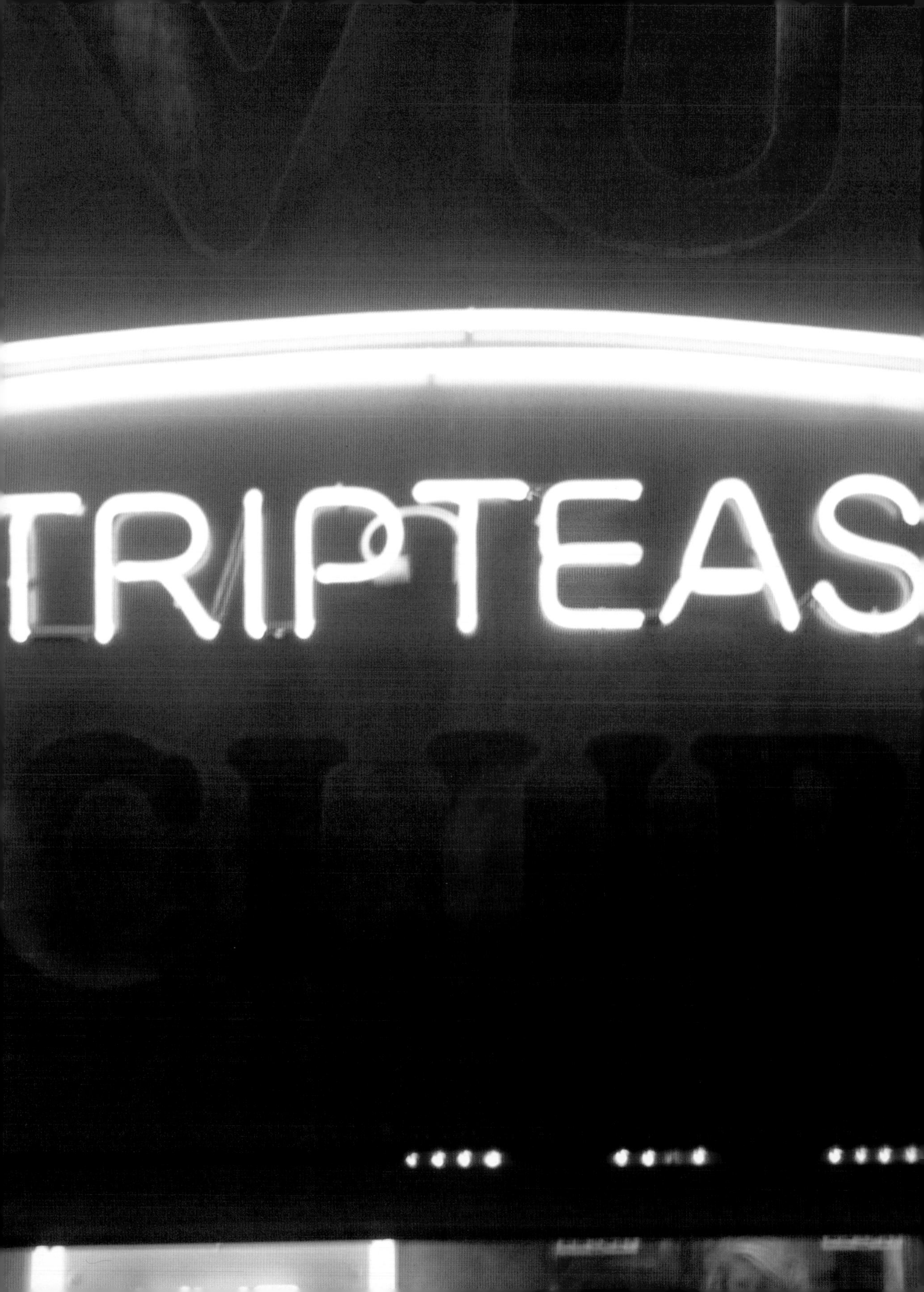
TRIPTEAS

5

This frosting can be tinted using natural food coloring. I prefer to use an edible paste coloring rather than a liquid because it doesn't affect the consistency of the frosting.

VANILLA BUTTERCREAM FROSTING

FOR 12 CUPCAKES

2¼ sticks unsalted butter, softened
5 cups confectioner's sugar
2 tbsp milk
1 tsp vanilla extract

In a large bowl, cream the butter, ideally using an electric hand mixer on medium speed. Blend in the sugar, one-quarter of it at a time, beating well after each addition. Beat in the milk and vanilla extract, and continue mixing until light and fluffy.

Keep the frosting covered until you are ready to use it.

Smooth the frosting onto the cupcakes using a small metal spatula. You can also create small spikes by quickly touching the frosting with the flat blade of the metal spatula.

Be careful when melting white chocolate because it is much more temperamental than semisweet.

CREAM CHEESE FROSTING

FOR 12 CUPCAKES

2oz white chocolate, broken
    into pieces
heaped ¾ cup cream cheese,
    softened
7 tbsp unsalted butter, softened
1 tsp vanilla extract
4¼ cups confectioner's sugar

Add the white chocolate pieces to a heatproof bowl and place over a saucepan of barely simmering water making sure the bowl does not touch the surface of the water. Stir until the chocolate melts and is smooth. Remove the bowl from the heat and leave to cool to room temperature.

In another bowl, using a wooden spoon or an electric hand mixer, beat together the cream cheese and butter until smooth. Then stir in the melted white chocolate and the vanilla extract. Gradually beat in the confectioner's sugar until the mixture is fluffy.

Smooth the frosting onto the cupcakes using a small metal spatula. You can also create small spikes by quickly touching the frosting with the flat blade of the metal spatula.

This recipe calls for raw egg whites. If you are worried about using raw eggs, you can buy reconstituted albumen powder instead.

ROYAL ICING

MAKES 1LB 2OZ

2 egg whites
1 tsp lemon juice
about 5 cups confectioner's sugar, sifted
edible food coloring paste (see page 159 for suppliers)

Add the egg whites to a bowl and stir in the lemon juice. Gradually add the sifted confectioner's sugar, mixing well after each addition.

Continue adding small amounts of confectioner's sugar until you achieve the desired consistency. For piping, the icing should be fairly stiff.

Edible food coloring paste is highly concentrated so only use a tiny amount. Dip a toothpick into the coloring paste. Mix well into the icing before adding more coloring paste to avoid streaks.

Use high-quality semisweet chocolate to make this rich chocolate buttercream frosting. It makes a great frosting for chocolate cupcakes or cakes.

CHOCOLATE FROSTING

FOR 12 CUPCAKES

1 cup less 2 tbsp light cream
8oz semisweet chocolate, finely
    chopped
3½ tbsp unsalted butter, softened

Heat the cream in a small saucepan, but do not allow it to boil.

Put the chocolate into a heatproof bowl and pour the hot cream through a fine sieve onto the chocolate. Gently stir the cream into the chocolate until the mixture is glossy. Carefully stir in the softened butter and leave the mixture to cool completely.

Once it is cool, beat until fluffy, ideally using an electric hand mixer.

Use this frosting as a filling for cupcakes or cakes, or for spreading on top. To achieve a dark glossy chocolate coating, you can use this without the final whipping.

FOR 12 MINI CUPCAKES YOU WILL NEED:

rose mold, approximately the same diameter as your cupcakes (see page 159 for suppliers)

cornstarch, for dusting

chocolate paste or "plastic," colored with red and pink edible food coloring paste (see page 159 for suppliers)

small paintbrush

boiled water, cooled

edible glitter in "disco red" and "plum perfection" (see page 159 for suppliers)

pastry bag fitted with a star tip

½ quantity Vanilla Buttercream or Cream Cheese Frosting (see pages 88–9), colored with red or pink edible food coloring pastes

12 mini cupcakes

VALENTINE'S DAY ROSE CUPCAKES

Dust the inside of the mold with a little cornstarch to stop the chocolate "plastic" from sticking.

Coat your fingertips with cornstarch, take a small ball of chocolate "plastic," and press it tightly into the mold.

Pop out the rose shape—it will not set hard so there is no need to leave it to dry.

Using a small dry paintbrush, brush the excess cornstarch off of the rose shapes, then lightly brush the surface with the cooled boiled water.

Dust generously with red or pink edible glitter. Shake off the excess, and leave to dry. Using a pastry bag fitted with a star tip, pipe spirals of frosting onto each cupcake and place a glittery rose on top to finish.

FOR 12 CUPCAKES
YOU WILL NEED:

cornstarch, for dusting

small rolling pin

2oz white ready-made gum
   paste (see page 159 for
   suppliers)

small dry paintbrush

edible rainbow dust in
   "Christmas red" (see page
   159 for suppliers)

boiled water, cooled

1 heaped cup desiccated
   coconut

small metal spatula

1 quantity Vanilla Buttercream
   or Cream Cheese Frosting
   (see pages 88–9), colored
   with green edible food
   coloring paste

12 chocolate or vanilla cupcake
   bases (see pages 16 and 66)

Dust a little cornstarch onto your work
surface and roll out the gum paste very
thinly, about ⅛ inch thick. To make the
ears, cut out 24 petal shapes, each
3½ inches long and ¾ inch at the
widest part. (You may want to make a
paper template to cut around.) Leave to
dry in the refrigerator for several hours,
or ideally overnight, until hard.

Using a small dry paintbrush, stain
one side of each ear with red edible
rainbow dust, leaving a white border.

Lightly paint the white areas only of
each ear on both sides with cooled
boiled water and immediately dip into
the desiccated coconut to coat. Leave
to dry for a few minutes.

Using a small metal spatula, spread
the frosting onto each cupcake. You can
create a spiky grass effect by tapping
the flat blade of the metal spatula onto
the frosting. Poke 2 ears into each
cupcake to finish.

BUNNY
CUPCAKES

FOR 12 CUPCAKES
YOU WILL NEED:

cornstarch, for dusting

small rolling pin

1½oz white ready-made
   gum paste (see page 159
   for suppliers)

6-inch square piece of
   waxed paper

½ cup Royal Icing (see page 90)

small paintbrush

boiled water, cooled

edible glitter in gold, blue, and
   red (see page 159 for
   suppliers)

small metal spatula

1 quantity Vanilla Buttercream
   or Cream Cheese Frosting
   (see pages 88–9), colored
   with violet edible food
   coloring paste (see page
   159 for suppliers)

12 chocolate or vanilla cupcake
   bases (see pages 16 and 66)

CROWN
CUPCAKES

Dust a little cornstarch onto your work surface to stop the gum paste from sticking to it. Roll out the gum paste to ¼ inch thick. Cut 12 strips, each 6 inches long and ½ inch wide. Press the two ends together to make a circle. Leave to dry in the refrigerator for a few hours, or ideally overnight, until hard.

Make a miniature pastry bag with the waxed paper by rolling it into a cone and folding the edges over. Fill with royal icing and snip off the tip. Pipe a row of small dots on top of the rim of the crown, holding the bag vertically with the tip close to the surface. Squeeze a little icing out, then push down and up sharply to finish.

Pipe a second row of dots on top of the first row in between the gaps, then more dots to build up the tips of the crown. Leave to dry for a few minutes.

Lightly brush the crown all over with the cooled boiled water and sprinkle with gold edible glitter. Use a small paintbrush to paint on additional colors as desired. Repeat with the remaining crowns and set aside.

Using a small metal spatula, spread the frosting on top of each cupcake. (If your frosting seems a little too thick, dip your metal spatula in hot water and this will make spreading easier.) Arrange a glittering crown on top of each frosted cupcake to finish.

**FOR 12 CUPCAKES
YOU WILL NEED:**

1 quantity Vanilla Buttercream
    or Cream Cheese Frosting
    (see pages 88–9), colored
    with peach edible food
    coloring paste
pastry bag fitted with a plain
    round tip
12 chocolate or vanilla cupcake
    bases (see pages 16 and 66)
edible diamonds, edible gold
    balls, sugar flowers, and
    edible glitter in gold
    to decorate
tweezers

Your frosting needs to flow freely and
not be too stiff. Fill the pastry bag
with frosting, twist the end tightly, and
squeeze gently until the frosting starts
to come through. Starting at the rim
farthest away from you, hold the pastry
bag at a 45° angle, pipe a dot, and stop
squeezing, tipping the bag vertically
toward the center of the cake.

Repeat around three-quarters of
the rim, then create a second row in
between the gaps, and keep repeating
until you reach the middle.

Continue piping dots down the back of
the cupcake to the rim. Repeat for the
remaining cupcakes.

Use tweezers to arrange your chosen
bling decorations carefully on top of
the frosting then dust lightly with edible
glitter in gold to finish. Repeat with the
remaining cupcakes.

BLING
CUPCAKES

**FOR 12 CUPCAKES
YOU WILL NEED:**

3½oz white chocolate, melted, colored with "skin-colored" edible pastes of your choice

squeeze bottle

beach bum mold (see page 159 for suppliers)

pastry bag fitted with a plain tip

1 quantity Vanilla Buttercream or Cream Cheese Frosting (see pages 88–9), colored with yellow, violet, or orange edible food coloring pastes

12 chocolate or vanilla cupcake bases (see pages 16 and 66)

small paintbrush

edible black food paint, or any color of your choice (see page 159 for suppliers)

CHEEKY CUPCAKES

Transfer the colored white chocolate to a squeeze bottle for easy use or simply spoon the melted chocolate into the beach bum molds, ensuring they are filled to the top. Tap the molds on the work surface to get rid of any air bubbles before leaving them in the refrigerator for 1 hour to set.

Fill the pastry bag with frosting, twist the end tightly, and squeeze gently until the frosting starts to come through. Hold the bag vertically and slowly pipe a ring of frosting around the rim of a cupcake. Then continue in a spiral until you reach the center. Stop squeezing, then push the bag down and up sharply to finish.

Remove the molds from the fridge and pop out the beach bums.

Using a small paintbrush, carefully paint on the bikini decoration using black edible paint (or the coloring of your choice). Leave to dry for a few minutes.

Place on top of the cupcake to finish. Repeat with the remaining molds and cupcakes.

FOR 12 CUPCAKES
YOU WILL NEED:

6-inch square piece of waxed
    paper
½ quantity Vanilla Buttercream
    or Cream Cheese Frosting,
    (see pages 88–9), leaving
    some white (for the noses),
    with half the remainder
    colored with beige edible
    food paste and the rest
    colored brown
12 chocolate or vanilla cupcake
    bases (see pages 16 and 66)
2 pastry bags fitted with plain
    round tips
24 chocolate "eyes" (see page
    159 for suppliers)
6 miniature marshmallows

Make a miniature pastry bag with the
waxed paper by rolling it into a cone
shape and folding the edges over. Fill
with the white frosting then snip off the
tip of the bag so the frosting flows out.
First, make the base of the nose by
piping a ¾-inch spiral of white frosting
above the rim on each cupcake.

Fill one of the pastry bags with beige-
colored frosting and the other with
brown-colored frosting, twist the ends
tightly, and squeeze gently until the
frosting starts to come through. Take the
beige pastry bag, hold at a 45° angle,
and pipe outward around half the rim of
a cupcake, squeezing a little and tilting
the bag upright to form the quills.

Now take the brown frosting and pipe
more spikes overlapping the beige
quills to form a second row. Repeat,
alternating the colors to cover the cake
until you reach the nose.

Place the chocolate "eyes" into position
above the nose.

Cut the corner off of a mini
marshmallow and place it on top of
the white frosting to form the tip of the
nose. Repeat the decoration with the
remaining cupcakes.

PORCUPINE
CUPCAKES

FOR 12 CUPCAKES
YOU WILL NEED:

small metal spatula

1 quantity Vanilla Buttercream
  or Cream Cheese frosting
  (see pages 88–9), colored
  with violet edible food
  coloring paste

12 chocolate or vanilla cupcake
  bases (see pages 16 and 66)

pastry bag fitted with a plain
  ¼-inch tip

½ quantity Vanilla Buttercream
  or Cream Cheese Frosting,
  1 tbsp colored with black
  edible food coloring paste
  (for the stigma), the
  remainder colored with
  orange edible food coloring
  paste

6-inch square piece of waxed
  paper

Using a small metal spatula, cover the top of each cupcake with a smooth layer of the violet-colored frosting.

Fill the pastry bag with orange frosting. Twist the end tightly and squeeze gently until the frosting starts to come through. Holding the bag at a 45° angle, start at the rim and pipe a petal shape by squeezing the bag across the cupcake toward the center. Twist upward to finish. Repeat around the cake to cover.

Now pipe a second layer on top of the first layer.

Make a miniature pastry bag with the waxed paper by rolling it into a cone shape and folding the edges over. Fill with black frosting then snip the tip off of the bag so the frosting flows out. Pipe tiny dots in the center of the cupcake to form the stigma, piling them to build up some height. Repeat the decoration with the remaining cupcakes.

SUMMER
FLOWER
CUPCAKES

FOR 12 CUPCAKES
YOU WILL NEED:

3½oz semisweet chocolate, melted
skull and crossbones molds (see page 159 for suppliers)
small paintbrush
edible glitter in silver and red (see page 159 for suppliers)
pastry bag fitted with a plain tip
1 quantity Vanilla Buttercream or Cream Cheese Frosting (see pages 88–9), colored with black edible food coloring paste
12 chocolate cupcake bases (see page 16)

Spoon the melted chocolate into the skull and crossbones molds, ensuring they are filled to the top. Tap the molds on the work surface to get rid of any air bubbles before leaving them in the refrigerator for 1 hour to set.

Remove the molds from the fridge and pop out the chocolate skull and crossbones. Using a small paintbrush, decorate with edible silver and red glitter as desired.

Fill the pastry bag with frosting, twist the end tightly, and squeeze gently until the frosting starts to come through. Hold the bag vertically and slowly pipe a ring of frosting around the edge of a cupcake, then continue in a spiral until you reach the center and the cupcake is covered. Stop the pressure, then push the bag down and up sharply to finish.

Set a skull and crossbones into the frosting on the cupcake. Repeat with the remaining cupcakes.

BLACK SKULL CAKES

FOR 12 CUPCAKES
YOU WILL NEED:

3½oz white chocolate, melted
   and colored with "skin-
   colored" edible food
   paste of your choice
squeeze bottle
torso mold (see page 159
   for suppliers)
pastry bag fitted with a plain tip
1 quantity Vanilla Buttercream
   or Cream Cheese Frosting
   (see pages 88–9), colored
   with caramel edible food
   coloring paste
¾ cup toffee bits
12 chocolate or vanilla cupcake
   bases (see pages 16 and 66)
edible confectioners' glaze,
   (see page 159 for suppliers)

Transfer the melted chocolate to a squeeze bottle for easy use or spoon it into the molds, ensuring you fill them to the top. Tap the molds on the work surface to get rid of any air bubbles before leaving them in the refrigerator for 1 hour to set.

Fill the pastry bag with frosting, twist the end tightly, and squeeze gently until the frosting starts to come through. Hold the bag vertically and slowly pipe a ring of frosting around the edge of a cupcake. Continue in a spiral until you reach the center. Stop the pressure, then push the bag down and up sharply to finish. Sprinkle toffee chips around the rim. Remove the molds from the refrigerator and pop the chocolate torsos out.

Spray or paint edible confectioners' glaze onto each chocolate torso to give a shiny finish then set one torso on top of each cupcake to decorate.

MAN CAKES

FOR 12 CUPCAKES
YOU WILL NEED:

¼ cup Royal Icing (see page 90), colored with "skin-colored" edible food coloring paste

dome-shaped silicone cupcake mold

1½ quantities Vanilla Buttercream or Cream Cheese Frosting (see pages 88–9), colored with "skin-colored" edible food coloring paste of your choice

small metal spatula

Make the nipples from 1 small disk and 1 small ball of royal icing and leave to set. Bake vanilla or chocolate cupcake bases (following the recipe on page 66 or 16) in the dome-shaped silicone molds without using paper baking cups. Cut each cupcake in half vertically.

Spread a thin layer of frosting inside one of the cut halves and sandwich the other half together. Using a small metal spatula, spread frosting all over the top of the cupcakes and smooth it over.

Place a nipple on top of each cake and serve on a tartlet pan or plate.

TITTY CAKES

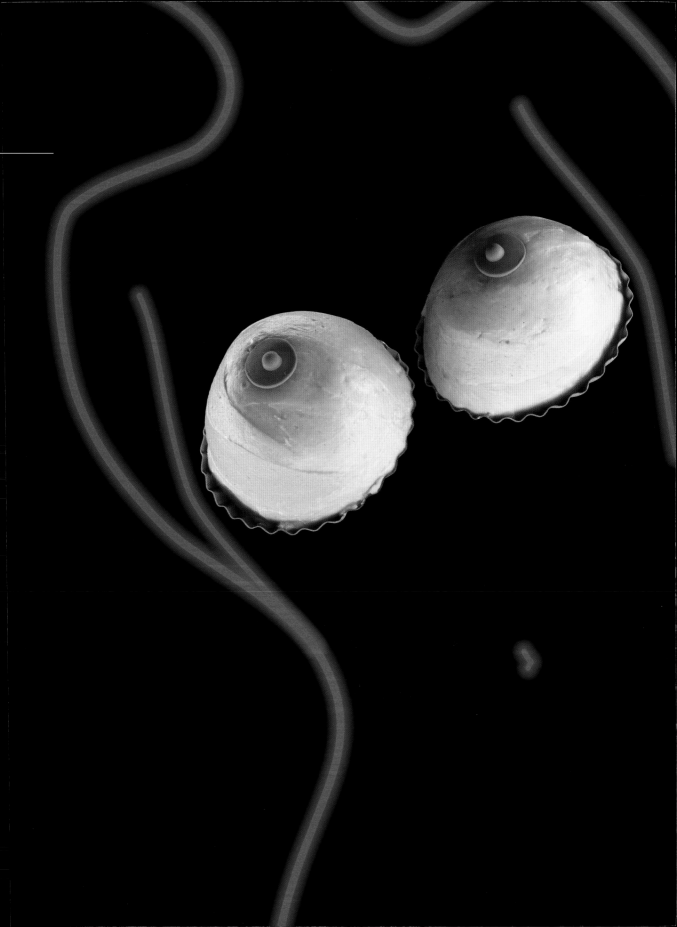

FOR 12 CUPCAKES
YOU WILL NEED:

3½oz white chocolate
12 dome-shaped chocolates
    (such as Lindor)
small paintbrush
edible rainbow dust in red (see
    page 159 for suppliers)
boiled water, cooled
edible glitter in blue, green, and
    black (see page 159 for
    suppliers)
1 quantity Vanilla Buttercream
    or Cream Cheese Frosting
    (see pages 88–9), colored
    with edible coloring pastes
12 chocolate or vanilla cupcake
    bases (see pages 16 and 66)
6-inch square piece of waxed
    paper
piping gel, colored with red
    edible coloring paste

POKE-IN-THE-EYE CUPCAKES

Melt the white chocolate in a heatproof bowl placed over a saucepan of barely simmering water, making sure the bowl does not touch the surface of the water. Dip the dome-shaped chocolates into the white chocolate until completely covered. Leave on a plate in the refrigerator to set.

After 2 hours, remove from the refrigerator. Using a small dry paintbrush, dust red edible rainbow dust onto the white chocolate eyeballs.

Lightly brush a circle of water on one side, then paint edible blue or green glitter over the wet circle. Paint the center with black edible glitter.

Using the tip of a small sharp knife, score from the center of the eyeball outward several times to create a veined effect. Spread colored frosting onto the cupcakes and place an eyeball on top of each one.

Make a miniature pastry bag with the waxed paper by rolling it into a cone shape and folding the edges over. Fill with red piping gel and snip off the tip of the bag so the gel flows out. Pipe the gel into the center of the eyeball and let it drizzle down over the frosting. Repeat with the remaining cupcakes.

FOR 12 CUPCAKES
YOU WILL NEED:

6 pieces of bubble wrap, each measuing 4 x 8 inches

7oz semisweet, milk, or white chocolate, melted

1 quantity Vanilla Buttercream or Cream Cheese Frosting (see pages 88–9)

12 chocolate cupcake bases (see page 16)

small paintbrush with soft bristles

edible rainbow dust in gold (see page 159 for suppliers)

edible glitter in gold (optional)

Wash and dry the bubble wrap and place it, bubbles facing up, on cookie sheets that will fit in your refrigerator. Pour the melted chocolate onto the bubble wrap, dividing the chocolate equally between each piece.

Use a knife to spread the chocolate evenly, then place in the refrigerator for 1 hour to set. Meanwhile, frost the cupcakes.

Once the chocolate has set, carefully peel off and discard the bubble wrap.

Use a small dry paintbrush to highlight areas of the chocolate honeycomb with gold edible rainbow dust.

Snap each chocolate piece into 4 so you have 24 pieces. Push 2 pieces into the frosting on each cupcake. To finish, if using, dust some edible glitter in gold down the sides of the frosting.

CHOCOLATE HONEYCOMB CUPCAKES

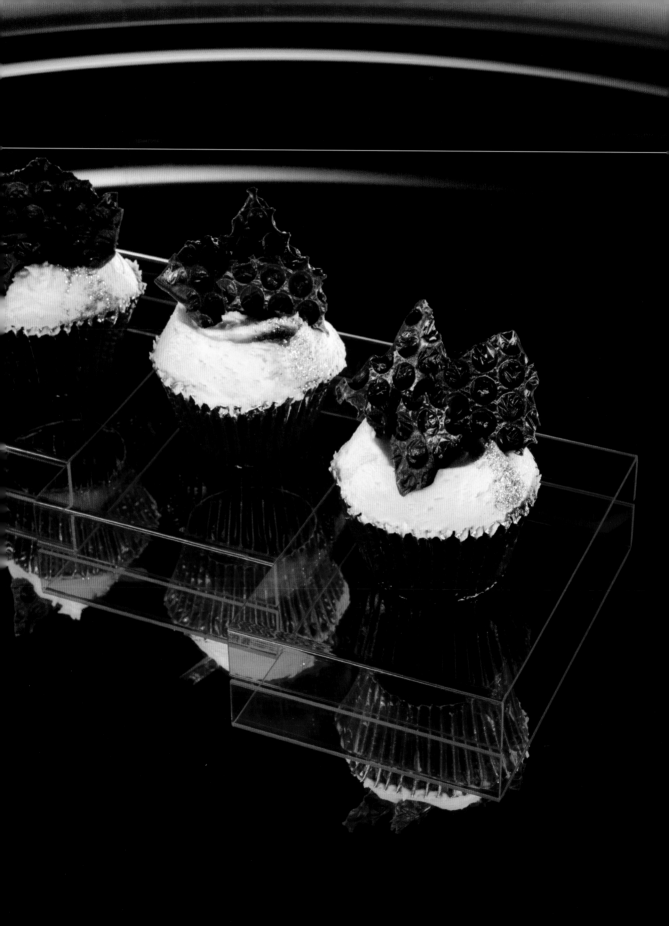

**FOR 12 CUPCAKES
YOU WILL NEED:**

cornstarch, for dusting

small rolling pin

1½oz white ready-made
    gum paste

snowflake cutter (see page 159
    for suppliers)

small paintbrush with soft
    bristles

boiled water, cooled

edible glitter in silver (see
    page 159 for suppliers)

pastry bag fitted with a plain tip

1 quantity Vanilla Buttercream
    or Cream Cheese Frosting
    (see pages 88–9), colored
    with red edible food coloring
    paste

12 chocolate or vanilla cupcake
    bases (see pages 16 and 66)

SNOWFLAKE CUPCAKES

Dust a little cornstarch onto your work surface to stop the gum paste from sticking to it, then roll it out to a thickness of about ⅛ inch.

Using a snowflake cutter, cut out 12 shapes and leave them to dry in the refrigerator for several hours, or ideally overnight, until hard.

Using a small paintbrush, lightly brush cooled boiled water all over the surface of a snowflake. Cover it with edible glitter and shake off the excess, then leave to dry for a few minutes. Repeat with the remaining snowflakes.

Fill the pastry bag with frosting, twist the end tightly, and squeeze gently until the frosting starts to come through. Hold the bag vertically and slowly pipe a ring of frosting around the edge of a cupcake, then continue in a spiral until you reach the center and the cupcake is covered. Stop the pressure, then push the bag down and up sharply to finish.

Frost the remaining cupcakes in the same way then position a glittery snowflake on top of each one.

**FOR 12 CUPCAKES
YOU WILL NEED:**

bauble mold (see page 159 for
   suppliers)
cornstarch, for dusting
1½oz white ready-made
   gum paste
small paintbrush
edible rainbow dust in gold (see
   page 159 for suppliers)
boiled water, cooled
edible glitter in gold (see
   page 159 for suppliers)
pastry bag with ¼-inch plain tip
1 quantity Vanilla Buttercream
   or Cream Cheese Frosting
   (see pages 88–9), colored
   with green edible food
   coloring paste
12 chocolate or vanilla cupcake
   bases (see pages 16 and 66)

CHRISTMAS TREE BAUBLE CUPCAKES

Dust the inside of the mold with a little cornstarch. Coat your fingertips with cornstarch, take a small ball of gum paste, and press it tightly into the bauble mold. Pop out the shape and repeat until you have 12 baubles.

Using a small dry paintbrush, brush the excess cornstarch off the bauble shapes. Leave them to set in the refrigerator for a few hours, or ideally overnight, until hard.

Once they have set, use a small paintbrush to paint the ornament "fixture" at the top with edible gold rainbow dust. Then lightly brush the rest of the bauble with the cooled boiled water, carefully avoiding the part you have painted with rainbow dust.

Sprinkle edible glitter over the bauble, shake off the excess, and leave to dry.

To create the Christmas tree effect, the frosting needs to be free-flowing and not too stiff. Fill the pastry bag with frosting, twist the end tightly, and squeeze gently until the frosting starts to come through.

Pipe a dot on the rim of the cupcake, stop squeezing, tip the bag vertically, and push the tip of the nozzle toward the center of the cupcake. Repeat around the rim, then create a second row in between the gaps and repeat until you reach the middle. Pipe a swirl in the center and arrange a bauble on top.

FOR 12 CUPCAKES
YOU WILL NEED:

cornstarch, for dusting

small rolling pin

2oz green ready-made
gum paste (see page 159
for suppliers)

small sharp knife

small paintbrush with soft
bristles

boiled water, cooled

edible glitter in "disco green,"
"yellow," and "super nova
purple" (see page 159 for
suppliers)

pastry bag fitted with a ¼-inch
plain tip

1 quantity Vanilla Buttercream
or Cream Cheese Frosting
(see pages 88–9), colored
with red, green, and/or
yellow edible food coloring
pastes

12 chocolate or vanilla cupcake
bases (see pages 16 and 66)

HOLLY LEAF
CUPCAKES

Dust a little cornstarch onto your work surface to stop the gum paste from sticking to it. Then roll out the gum paste to ⅛ inch in thickness.

Using the tip of a small sharp knife, carefully cut out 12 holly leaves. (You may find it easier to make a paper template first to cut around.) Leave them to dry in the refrigerator for several hours, or ideally overnight, until hard.

Using a small paintbrush, lightly brush the cooled boiled water over the surface of the holly leaves. Cover with edible glitter and shake off the excess, then leave them to dry for a few minutes.

Fill the pastry bag with frosting, twist the end tightly, and squeeze gently until the frosting starts to come through. Hold the bag vertically and slowly pipe a ring of frosting around the edge of a cupcake. Continue in a spiral until you reach the center. Stop the pressure, then push the bag down and up sharply to finish.

Poke the holly leaf into the top of the frosted cupcake. Frost the remaining cupcakes in the same way and arrange a holly leaf on top of each to finish.

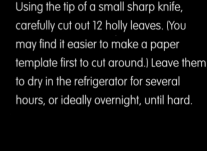

BARGAIN
BOOKS
&
Erotica
DOWNSTAIRS

6

If you are a fan of chewy cookies I can guarantee these will become your new favorite. The combination of the melted toffee bits, semisweet chocolate chunks, and the freshly baked cookie dough is irresistible. This is a cookie to eat straight from the oven, ideally with honeycomb ice cream.

DOUBLE CHOCOLATE TOFFEE COOKIES

MAKES 14 COOKIES

1³⁄₈ sticks unsalted butter, softened
²⁄₃ cups soft brown sugar
1 egg
1¼ cups all-purpose flour
½ tsp baking powder
3 tbsp unsweetened cocoa powder
3½oz semisweet chocolate chunks
   or ½ cup chocolate chips
heaped ½ cup toffee bits

Preheat the oven to 400°F, and line a cookie sheet with a silicone baking mat or parchment paper.

In a large bowl, cream the butter and sugar together. Add the egg, then sift in the flour, baking powder, and cocoa powder. Mix until well combined. Fold in the chocolate chunks and toffee bits.

Place spoonfuls of the cookie dough onto the cookie sheet. Leave space between them because they will spread out while baking. Bake for 12–15 minutes, or until golden brown at the edges but still soft in the middle.

Leave to cool on the cookie sheet for 5 minutes, then lift the individual cookies onto a wire rack to cool completely.

These fruity flavored soft-dough cookies will be a hit with everybody. If you make them slightly smaller and then present them in a decorative bag or put them in a beautiful box they make an attractive and festive gift.

ORANGE & WHITE CHOCOLATE CHIP COOKIES

MAKES ABOUT 36 SMALL COOKIES

1⅛ sticks unsalted butter, softened
heaped ¾ cup superfine sugar
2 tsp liquid honey
2 tbsp milk
1 tsp vanilla extract
grated zest and juice of 1 orange
2 cups self-rising flour
1 tsp ground cinnamon
½ cup white chocolate chips

Preheat the oven to 400°F, and line 2 cookie sheets with silicone baking mats or parchment paper.

In a large bowl, cream the butter, sugar, and honey together until pale and fluffy. Beat in the milk, vanilla extract, and the orange zest and juice. Sift the flour and cinnamon together in another bowl then stir this into the mixture. Then fold in the white chocolate chips.

Place heaped teaspoonfuls of the cookie dough onto the cookie sheets. Leave space between them because the cookies will spread out while baking. Bake for about 10 minutes, or until golden brown at the edges but still soft in the middle.

Leave to cool on the cookie sheets for 5 minutes, then lift the individual cookies onto a wire rack to cool completely.

These traditional Dutch cookies, also known as "speculaas," are baked on St. Nicholas Eve (December 5th). They make perfect Christmas cookies because you can cut them out into many different shapes and decorate them any way you like using royal icing. Or, you can keep them simple, as I have done here, with a delicious roasted almond topping.

WINDMILL COOKIES

MAKES 40–50 COOKIES, DEPENDING ON SIZE

2¼ sticks unsalted butter, softened
2 cups soft brown sugar
1 egg
½ tsp almond extract
½ tsp vanilla extract
2¾ cups all-purpose flour
1 tsp baking powder
½ tsp ground cloves
½ tsp ground cinnamon
½ tsp freshly grated nutmeg
1 cup finely ground almonds
1 egg, beaten
½ cup sliced almonds

Preheat the oven to 400°F, and line several cookie sheets with silicone baking mats or parchment paper.

In a large bowl, cream the butter and sugar together until pale and fluffy.

Beat in the egg, then stir in the almond and vanilla extracts. In another bowl, sift the flour, baking powder, and spices together. Add this to the creamed mixture followed by the ground almonds and stir until you have smooth dough.

With a rolling pin, roll the dough out on a floured surface to a ¼-inch thickness. Using a cookie cutter, cut out shapes and transfer them to the cookie sheets. Brush each cookie with beaten egg and then scatter with the sliced almonds.

Bake for 13–15 minutes, or until golden. Leave to cool on the cookie sheets for 5 minutes, then lift the individual cookies onto a wire rack to cool completely.

These cookies will keep well in an airtight container.

It is amazing how this traditional and iconic cake can be transformed into a cookie. These chunky soft cookies are bursting with the rich cherry and chocolate flavors of the cake—the only thing missing is the cream. But I think a drizzle of fresh cream is the perfect accompaniment for these cookies. They're the ideal dessert cookie!

BLACK FOREST SOFT COOKIES

MAKES 12–15

1 cup all-purpose flour
¼ cup unsweetened cocoa powder
1 tsp baking powder
4oz semisweet chocolate, broken into pieces
5 tbsp unsalted butter, softened
heaped ½ cup dark brown sugar
1 large egg
1¼ cups dried cherries, soaked overnight in 2 tbsp kirsch
5oz semisweet chocolate chunks
light cream, to serve

Preheat the oven to 400°F, and line 3–4 cookie sheets with slicone baking mats or parchment paper.

Sift the flour, unsweetened cocoa powder, and baking powder together into a medium-sized bowl.

Melt the semisweet chocolate in a large heatproof bowl placed over a saucepan of barely simmering water, making sure the bowl does not touch the surface of the water. Then leave to cool a little.

In a large bowl, ideally using an electric hand mixer, cream the butter with the sugar until pale and fluffy, then add the egg. Fold in the melted chocolate followed by the sifted dry ingredients, then the drained cherries and the chocolate chunks. The cookie dough will be very sticky, but this is fine.

Scoop 1½ tablespoons for each cookie onto the cookie sheets, leaving enough space between them to spread during baking. Press down lightly on each cookie with a fork.

Bake for 18–20 minutes, or until the cookies are soft but starting to firm up on top. It is important to remove them from the oven while they are still soft. Leave them to cool on the cookie sheets for 7–8 minutes, then lift the individual cookies onto a wire rack to cool completely. Serve with a drizzle of cream.

If you like chocolate, these cookies will become your "péché mignon" (indulgence)! They are so rich and chewy, coated with melted marshmallow... what else could you possibbly need?

DOUBLE CHOCOLATE & MARSHMALLOW COOKIES

MAKES 24 COOKIES

3oz semisweet chocolate, broken
   into pieces
1⅛ sticks unsalted butter, softened
1 cup + 1 tbsp soft brown sugar
1 egg
¼ cup milk
1 tsp vanilla extract
1¼ cups all-purpose flour
1 cup unsweetened cocoa powder
1 tsp baking powder
5oz semisweet chocolate chunks or
   1 scant cup semisweet chocolate
   chips
heaped ¾ cup white marshmallows
2 tsp water

Preheat the oven to 400°F, and line 2 cookie sheets with silicone baking mats or parchment paper.

Melt the chocolate in a heatproof bowl placed over a saucepan of barely simmering water making sure the bowl does not touch the surface of the water. Heat until completely melted and set aside to cool.

In a large bowl, cream the butter and sugar together until smooth. Add the egg, milk, and vanilla extract, and combine. Stir in the cooled melted chocolate and mix until smooth. Sift in the flour, cocoa powder, and baking powder then stir in the chocolate chunks or chips.

Place tablespoonfuls of the cookie dough onto the cookie sheets. Leave space between them because they will spread out during baking. Flatten them slightly with the back of a spoon that has been dipped in water. Bake for 12 minutes, or until firm to the touch.

Leave to cool on the cookie sheets for 5 minutes, then lift the individual cookies onto a wire rack to cool completely.

Place the marshmallows in a small saucepan over low heat. Add the water and stir until melted. Drizzle over the cooled cookies.

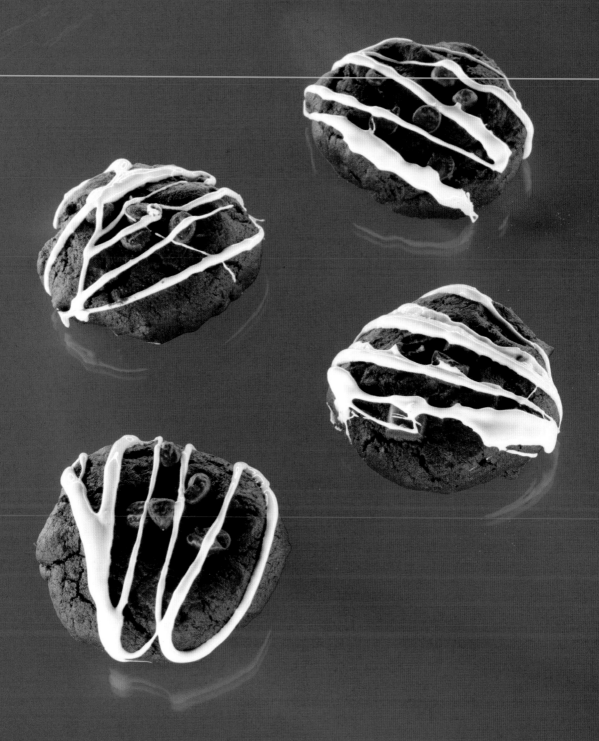

These delicious, spicy Indian-inspired cookies
are full of goodness and flavor.

CHAI TEA COOKIES

MAKES 28 COOKIES

2 sticks unsalted butter, softened
1¼ cups soft brown sugar
2 egg yolks
1 tbsp chai tea
½ tsp crushed roasted cardamom
   seeds
1 tsp vanilla extract
1½ cups whole-wheat flour
1 tsp baking powder
1 cup rolled oats
heaped ¾ cup golden raisins

Preheat the oven to 400°F, and line
2 cookie sheets with silicone baking
mats or parchment paper.

In a large bowl, cream the butter and
sugar together until light and fluffy. Beat
in the egg yolks, chai tea, cardamom
seeds, and vanilla extract. Sift in the
flour and baking powder, adding the
whole-wheat left behind in the sifter as
well, then add the oats. Stir to combine,
then fold in the golden raisins.

Place spoonfuls of the cookie dough on
the cookie sheets. Leave space between
them because they will spread while
baking. Bake for 15 minutes, or until
golden brown but still soft in the middle.

Leave to cool on the cookie sheets for
5 minutes, then lift the individual cookies
onto a wire rack to cool completely.

These nutty cookies are great served with fresh mint tea. Lemon oil can be found in most supermarkets and makes a real difference to the flavor.

LEMON PISTACHIO COOKIES

MAKES 28 COOKIES

7 tbsp unsalted butter, softened
½ tsp grated lemon zest
1 cup golden superfine sugar
2 eggs
2 tbsp milk
2 tsp pistachio paste
2 drops of lemon oil
2 cups all-purpose flour
1½ tsp baking powder
½ cup pistachio nuts, shelled
    and roughly chopped
confectioner's sugar, to dust

Preheat the oven to 400°F, and line 2 cookie sheets with silicone baking mats or parchment paper.

In a large bowl, blend the butter with lemon zest. Add the sugar and beat well until creamy. Beat in the eggs, milk, pistachio paste, and lemon oil, until well combined.

Sift in the flour and baking powder together and fold into the mixture, followed by the pistachio nuts.

Drop teaspoonfuls of the cookie dough onto the cookie sheets, spaced well apart, and flatten with the base of a spoon that has been dipped in cold water. Bake for 8–10 minutes, or until lightly golden.

Leave the cookies to cool on the cookie sheets for 5 minutes, then lift the individual cookies onto a wire rack to cool completely.

Lightly dust with confectioner's sugar just before serving.

I am lucky enough to visit the islands of Hawaii quite often, and my treat there will be anything made with their local macadamia nuts. These cookies are inspired by this favorite destination.

WHITE CHOCOLATE, MACADAMIA NUT & CRANBERRY COOKIES

MAKES 20 COOKIES

2 cups self-rising flour

heaped ¾ cup superfine sugar

¾ cup whole rolled oats

1⅛ sticks unsalted butter

2 tbsp light corn syrup

2 tbsp milk

3½oz white chocolate
    broken into pieces

¾ cup macadamia nuts,
    roughly chopped

scant ½ cup dried cranberries

vanilla ice cream and light corn
    syrup, to serve

Preheat the oven to 400°F, and line 2 cookie sheets with a silicone baking mat or parchment paper.

In a large bowl, mix together the flour, sugar, and oats. Cut the butter into the flour mixture until resembles coarse crumbs. Add the light corn syrup and milk, and combine. Stir in the white chocolate, nuts, and cranberries.

Place spoonfuls of the cookie dough onto the cookie sheets. Leave space between them because they will spread out during baking. Flatten the cookies slightly with a spoon that has been dipped in cold water. Bake for 15 minutes, or until golden brown.

Leave to cool on the cookie sheets for 5 minutes, then lift the individual cookies onto a wire rack to cool completely.

These cookies are amazing served with vanilla ice cream with a drizzle of light corn syrup.

7

NUTTY & CHOCOLATEY CUPCAKES

FRUITY CUPCAKES

RICH & SPICY CUPCAKES

GUILT-FREE CUPCAKES

STYLING CUPCAKES

COOKIES

BARS & BISCOTTI

My friend Laury, who is obsessed with anything Italian, introduced me to this recipe. She bakes them in the buildup to Thanksgiving and also serves them with a spicy Christmas coffee, just to put you in the mood.

PUMPKIN BISCOTTI

MAKES APPROXIMATELY 60

1 cup 1-inch cubes peeled
  pumpkin flesh
2 tbsp unsalted butter
2 cups toasted pecans,
  coarsely chopped
3²/3 cups all-purpose flour
2 cups less 2 tbsp brown sugar
2 tsp baking powder
2 tsp mixed spice
2 large eggs, lightly beaten

Steam the pumpkin cubes for 15–20 minutes until soft, then leave them to drain in a sieve over a bowl to remove as much moisture as possible. Mash puree the pumpkin and allow it to coo

Preheat the oven to 400°F, and line 2 cookie sheets with silicone baking mats or parchment paper.

Melt the butter in a skillet and add the pecans. Cook, stirring constantly, until the nuts are lightly browned. Remove from the heat, and leave to cool.

Meanwhile, in a large bowl combine the flour, sugar, baking powder, and mixed spice. In another bowl, combine the pumpkin, eggs, and vanilla extrac stirring well with a wire whisk. Slowly add the pumpkin mixture to the flour mixture, stirring until the dry ingredien are moistened. (The mixture will initiall be very crumbly, but will gradually become moist after stirring.) Add the nuts to the mixture and stir in.

Lightly flour your work surface then tip the dough onto it. Coat your hands lightly with flour and divide the dough into 6 portions. Shape each portion into a log 12 inches long and flatten it slightly. Arrange these about 3 inches apart on the cookie sheets.

Bake for 25 minutes, then remove from the oven and leave the logs to cool for 15 minutes.

Using a serrated knife, cut each log crosswise into ½-inch slices. Return these to the prepared cookie sheets, and bake for another 15 minutes. Allov the biscotti to cool completely on a wire

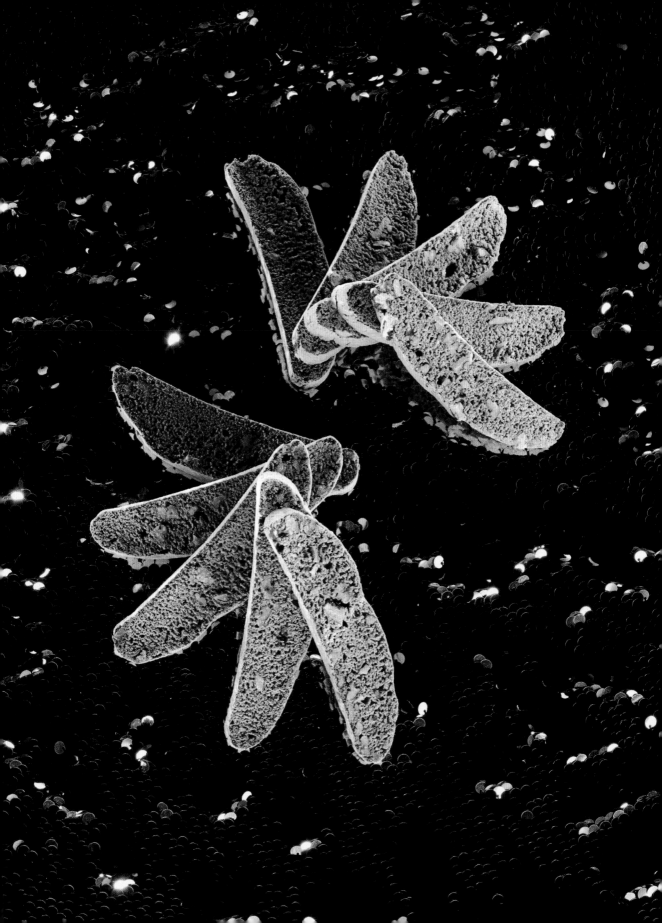

I was very skeptical about my friend Paul Feig's brownie recipe but after tasting them I am a complete convert! The rich chocolate flavor is boosted by the espresso while the candied ginger cuts right through the sweetness.

ESPRESSO BROWNIES WITH CANDIED GINGER

MAKES 12 BROWNIES

1¾ sticks unsalted butter, plus extra
    for greasing
7oz semisweet chocolate, broken
    into pieces
4 eggs
1 cup golden superfine sugar
2 tbsp espresso or very strong
    instant coffee
1½ cups + 1 tbsp all-purpose flour,
    sifted
3oz candied ginger, chopped

Preheat the oven to 400°F, and line a 10 x 8-inch baking pan with buttered parchment paper.

Place the chocolate and butter in a large heatproof bowl over a saucepan of barely simmering water, making sure the bowl does not touch the surface of the water. Heat, stirring until smooth and completely melted. Remove from the heat and half-cool.

In a large bowl, beat the eggs and sugar, ideally using an electric hand mixer, until the mixture is pale. Beat in the espresso followed by the half-cooled chocolate mixture. Fold in the flour followed by the ginger.

Pour the batter into the prepared baking pan. Bake for 20–25 minutes, or until crisp on top but still slightly gooey inside. Leave to cool completely in the pan then cut into bars.

These very light, chewy treats are great for kids to make and eat. They are also always a big hit at a school bake sale.

MARSHMALLOW RICE BARS

MAKES 24 SQUARES

3½ tbsp unsalted butter, plus extra
  for greasing
2 heaped cups white
  marshmallows
6 cups crisped rice cereal

FOR THE TOPPING

heaped ½ cup white marshmallows
4 tsp water
heaped ½ cup pink marshmallows
3oz white chocolate, melted

Place the butter in a large saucepan over low heat. Add the marshmallows and stir until melted and well blended in. Cook for 2 minutes longer, stirring constantly. Remove from the heat. When the mixture has cooled, stir in the cereal until it is all well coated.

Butter a 12 x 8-inch baking pan. Using a buttered spatula or sheet of waxed paper, press the mixture evenly and firmly into the prepared pan.

To make the topping: in a small saucepan, melt the white marshmallows with 2 teaspoons of water over very low heat, stirring constantly. Drizzle this mixture all over the top of the cereal layer. Repeat this step with the pink marshmallows. Finally drizzle the melted white chocolate all over the top to finish.

Chill until set, then cut into 2-inch squares to serve.

Ladyfingers have been around for centuries. Light and delicious, they have long been a favorite of Parisian ladies to accompany their flutes of Champagne. In fact, these raspberry versions are a perfect accompaniment to rosé Champagne. Clink, clink!

RASPBERRY LADYFINGERS

MAKES 30–35 LADYFINGERS

4 eggs, separated
¾ cup golden superfine sugar
a few drops of pink food coloring
2 drops of natural raspberry
    flavoring
heaped ¾ cup all-purpose flour
½ tsp baking powder
confectioner's sugar, to dust

Preheat the oven to 400°F, and line two 18 x 12-inch cookie sheets with silicone baking mats or parchment paper.

In a large and scrupulously clean bowl, beat the egg whites, ideally using an electric hand mixer on high, until soft peaks form. Slowly add 2 tablespoons of the sugar and continue beating until the mixture is stiff and glossy.

In another bowl, beat the egg yolks with the remaining sugar until thick and very pale in color. (Using an electric hand mixer really helps achieve a good result here.) Add the pink food coloring and raspberry flavoring to the mixture.

Sift the flour and baking powder together. Fold half the egg whites into the egg yolk mixture, then fold in the flour, followed by the remaining egg whites, being careful not to knock out too much of the air that you have painstakingly beaten in.

Transfer the mixture to a pastry bag fitted with ¾-inch plain tip. Pipe the mixture into fingers about 3 inches long on the cookie sheets, leaving a 1½-inch space between the fingers. Liberally dust with confectioner's sugar, leave to rest for 2 minutes, then dust again.

Bake in the oven for about 8 minutes until golden brown. Leave to cool on the cookie sheets for 5 minutes, then lift the individual fingers onto wire racks to cool completely.

These delicious treats are popular with the health-conscious because are they packed with goodness and will give you that vavavoom you need to start the day.

OAT & FRUIT BAR WITH YOGURT TOPPING

MAKES 10 BARS

7 tbsp unsalted butter, plus extra
  for greasing
2 tbsp sunflower seeds
2 tbsp pumpkin seeds
2 tbsp flax seeds
3 tbsp light corn syrup
2 bananas, peeled and mashed
1¼ cups rolled oats
1 cup dried mixed fruit

FOR THE YOGURT TOPPING

1¼ cups confectioner's sugar, sifted
¼ cup plain yogurt

Preheat the oven to 400°F. Grease a shallow 8-inch square baking pan and line the bottom with parchment paper.

Roughly chop all the seeds.

Melt the butter in a saucepan and stir in the light corn syrup. Add the chopped seeds and mashed bananas, together with the rolled oats and dried fruit. Mix together well.

Spoon the mixture into the prepared pan and level the surface. Bake for about 30 minutes or until golden brown. Leave to cool in the pan.

To make the Yogurt Topping: mix the confectioner's sugar with the yogurt. If it is too thick, add a little more yogurt.

Drizzle on top of the cooled oat bars. Leave to set and cut into squares and then into triangles with a sharp knife.

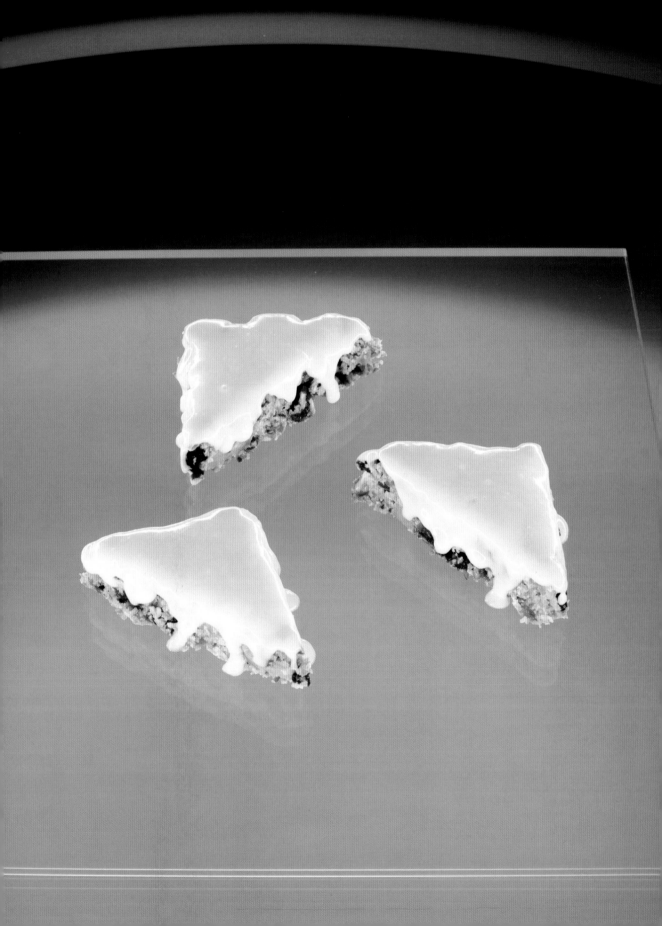

This classic shortbread recipe is perfect for adding icing. The technique here is to use layers of ready-made colored easy-roll fondant, but you can pipe them with royal icing (see page 90), too. By making a little hole in them as they come out of the oven you can turn them into hanging ornaments for Christmas or other occasions. The exact baking time will depend on the size and final shape of your shortbread, so keep an eye on it while it is baking. When using gum paste, always remember to cover it with plastic wrap when not using, because it dries out very rapidly.

ICED SHORTBREAD

MAKES 36–40 COOKIES, DEPENDING ON SIZE

2½ sticks + 1 tbsp unsalted butter
4 cups all-purpose flour
¾ cup superfine sugar
1 egg
2 tsp milk
1 tsp vanilla extract

FOR THE ICING
8oz ready-made gum paste in a selection of colors (see page 159 for suppliers)
scant ⅔ cups cornstarch
3 tbsp sieved apricot jam, warmed

Preheat the oven to 400°F, and line 2 cookie sheets with silicone baking mats or parchment paper.

Rub the butter into the flour with your fingertips, add the other ingredients, and work them in until they bind together to form a smooth dough. Don't overknead it!

Roll the dough out on a floured surface to a thickness of about ¼ inch. Using cookie cutters, cut out your favorite shapes. Reroll the trimmings and use them to cut out more shapes.

Place the cookies on the cookie sheets and set them on the middle rack of the oven. Bake for 12–15 minutes, keeping an eye on them while they are baking, until they are light golden in color.

To decorate the cookies, roll out the gum paste as thinly as possible, dusting it with the cornstarch to stop it from sticking to your work surface.

Cut out your chosen shapes from the rolled gum paste. Brush the warmed apricot jam onto each cookie and gently place a layer of gum paste on top. Use a small brush dipped in boiling water to stick layers of gum paste together.

These little French treats are a good alternative to cookies. You can finish them with any dried fruits and nuts on top. I like mine exotic-looking and glamorous, so flakes of edible gold leaf are a must.

WHITE CHOCOLATE MENDIANTS

MAKES ABOUT 18

7oz good-quality white chocolate, broken into pieces
1 cup assorted dried exotic fruits and nuts
a few flakes of edible gold leaf, to decorate (optional)

Line a large cookie sheet with parchment paper.

Gently melt the white chocolate in a heatproof bowl placed over a saucepan of barely simmering water, making sure the bowl does not touch the surface of the water.

Place teaspoonfuls of the chocolate on the paper and smooth into 2-inch disks. Working quickly, scatter the dried fruits and nuts onto the disks, and then flakes of the edible gold leaf, if using.

Leave for at least 30 minutes in the refrigerator to set before serving.

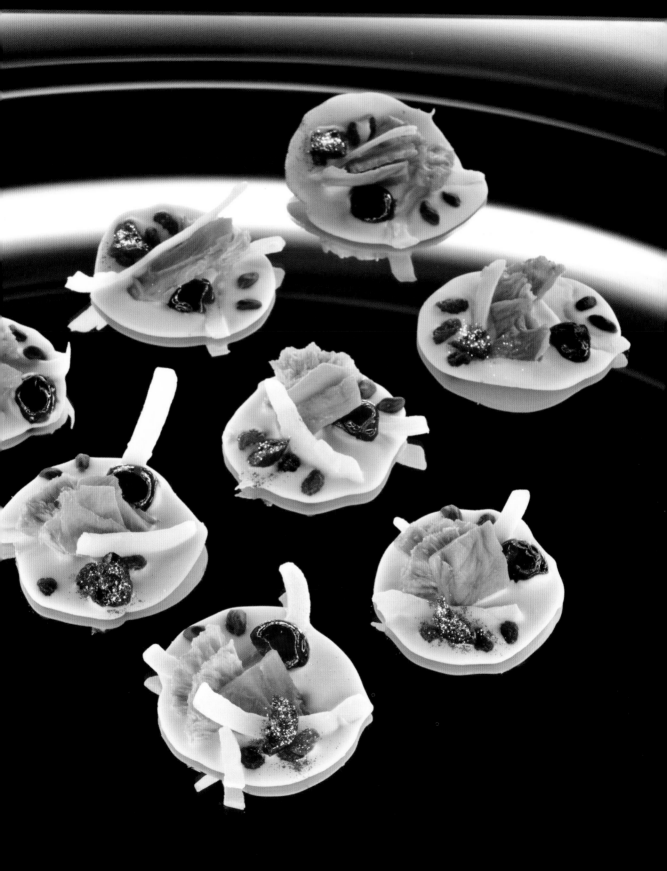

These are delicious served warm with crème fraîche and a drizzle of maple syrup. Always use pure maple syrup, not flavored syrup, or Mr. Cox will beat you up!

MAPLE PECAN STICKY BARS

MAKES 12

FOR THE FILLING
1¾ cups pecans, roughly chopped
scant ½ cup pure maple syrup
1 heaped cup soft brown sugar
2 tbsp whipping cream
1⅜ sticks unsalted butter
½ tsp vanilla extract

FOR THE CRUST
7 tbsp unsalted butter, softened,
    plus extra for greasing
⅓ cup golden superfine sugar
1 egg yolk
1⅓ cups all-purpose flour

Preheat the oven to 400°F, and butter a 9 x 9 x 2-inch square baking pan.

Toast the pecans in the oven for 5 minutes, then set aside to cool.

To make the crust: ideally using a stand mixer or an electric hand mixer, beat together the butter, sugar, and egg yolk until blended. Add the flour and beat until a soft dough forms. Gather the dough together and press it into the bottom of the pan and ¾ inch up the sides. Bake for about 18–20 minutes, or until golden. Remove from the oven, but leave the oven on. Set the crust aside to cool while you make the filling.

To make the filling: in a medium saucepan, combine all the ingredients except the nuts and vanilla extract. Bring to a boil, stirring until the butter melts and the mixture is smooth. Boil for 30 seconds. Remove from the heat and stir in the nuts and vanilla extract.

Pour the hot filling onto the cooled crust, and bake for about 15 minutes, or until the filling is bubbling in the center.

Remove from the oven and leave to cool completely in the pan to allow the filling to become firm. Then place in the refrigerator to chill for at least 1 hour and up to 2 hours.

When chilled, cut into bars with a large sharp knife.

The combination of the salted peanuts and the dark chocolate really works very well here, and the frosting makes these brownies very rich and indulgent. I like cutting them into bite-sized pieces—a good excuse to eat more of them!

PEANUT BUTTER & FUDGE BROWNIES

MAKES ABOUT 20 BROWNIES, DEPENDING ON SIZE

1½ sticks unsalted butter
10oz semisweet chocolate, broken into pieces
1¾ cups golden superfine sugar
1½ tsp vanilla extract
4 large eggs
heaped ¾ cup all-purpose flour
1¼ cups roasted salted peanuts, coarsely chopped

FOR THE FROSTING

1 cup chunky peanut butter
7 tbsp unsalted butter, softened
1¼ cups confectioner's sugar
1 tbsp milk
1 tsp vanilla extract

FOR THE GANACHE

3oz semisweet chocolate, broken into pieces
confectioner's sugar, to dust

Preheat the oven to 400°F, and line a 13 x 9 x 2-inch baking pan with foil or parchment paper.

Place the butter and chocolate in a large saucepan over very low heat. Continue stirring until they are melted and smooth. Remove from the heat.

Whisk in the sugar and vanilla extract, followed by the eggs, one at a time. Then fold in the flour followed by the nuts.

Spread the mixture in the prepared pan and bake for 25–30 minutes, or until a skewer inserted into center comes out with moist crumbs attached. Set aside to cool in the pan.

To make the Frosting; in a medium bowl, ideally using an electric hand mixer, beat the peanut butter with half the ordinary butter until blended. Then beat in the confectioner's sugar, followed by the milk and vanilla extract. Spread the frosting onto the cooled brownies.

To make the Ganache; melt the semisweet chocolate with the remaining butter in a heatproof bowl over a saucepan of simmering water, making sure the bowl does not touch the surface of the water. Allow to cool slightly, then drizzle the mixture onto the layer of frosting. Dust with confectioner's sugar before cutting into squares.

These old-fashioned cookies are perfect with tea or coffee. The combination of the rye flour and the molasses gives them a rich taste and the melted fudge provides a lovely sticky marbled effect.

MOLASSES CRINKLES

MAKES 28 COOKIES

1½ sticks unsalted butter, softened
1¼ cups soft brown sugar
1 egg
2 tbsp molasses
1½ cups rye flour
2 tsp baking powder
¼ tsp salt
½ tsp ground cloves
1 tsp ground cinnamon
1 tsp ground ginger
4oz fudge, diced
2 tbsp granulated sugar, for dipping

In a large bowl, ideally using an electric hand mixer, beat together the butter, sugar, egg, and molasses.

In another bowl, sift together the flour, baking powder, salt, and spices. Gradually add this to the butter mixture, followed by the diced fudge. Place in the refrigerator to chill for 20 minutes.

Preheat the oven to 400°F, and line 1 or 2 cookie sheets with parchment paper.

Roll the chilled dough in your hands to make 1¼-inch balls.

Dip their tops in the sugar and arrange them, sugar-side up and 3¼ inches apart, on the cookie sheets.

Bake for 10–12 minutes, or until just set but not hard. Allow the cookies to cool on the sheets before removing.

Named after the city of Nanaimo, British Columbia, these are said by some to be the national dessert of Canada. I like eating these irresistible bars at room temperature because they are then creamier and richer.

NANAIMO BARS

MAKES 10 BARS

FOR THE FIRST LAYER
¼ cup + 1 tbsp sugar
2 tbsp unsweetened cocoa powder, sifted
1¼ cups graham cracker crumbs
¾ cup desiccated coconut
½ cup walnuts, finely chopped
1⅛ sticks unsalted butter, melted

FOR THE SECOND LAYER
3½ tbsp butter, softened
2 tbsp custard powder (or instant vanilla pudding mix)
2 cups confectioner's sugar
a little warm water (optional)

FOR THE THIRD LAYER
5oz semisweet chocolate, broken into pieces
3½ tbsp unsalted butter

Line a shallow 8-inch square baking pan with parchment paper.

To make the first layer: in a large bowl, mix all the ingredients together except the butter. Pour in the melted butter and combine. Using the back of a spoon, press this into the pan and chill in the refrigerator for 15 minutes to set.

To make the second layer: cream the butter with the custard powder, ideally with an electric hand mixer, until fluffy. Then add the confectioner's sugar a little at a time. Add a little warm water if it gets too stiff. Smooth the creamy mixture on top of the chilled crust, and return to the refrigerator for 15 minutes to set.

To make the third layer: melt the chocolate and butter in a heatproof bowl over a saucepan of simmering water until smooth and glossy, making sure the base of the bowl does not touch the water. Let it cool slightly, then pour over the custard layer and smooth with a metal spatula. Chill for a further 15 minutes, or until set.

Remove the pan from the refrigerator 30 minutes before serving to allow to soften slightly, then cut into bars with a large sharp knife.

Cake Craft Shop
7 Chatterton Road
Bromley
Kent BR2 9QW
UK
www.cakecraftshop.co.uk
Tel. 011 44 1732 463573

*Supplier of edible food coloring
pastes; edible glaze spray, and
sugar decorations and flowers.*

Candy Direct, Inc.
745 Design Court, Suite 602
Chula Vista, CA 91911
Tel. 619-216-0116
www.candydirect.com

*Online store for all types of
candies.*

FPC Sugarcraft
www.fpcsugarcraft.co.uk
Tel. 100 44 117 9853249

*International supplier of lacy
panties, rose, skull, bauble,
beach bum, and torso-shaped
silicone rubber molds.*

Global Sugar Art
Tel. 1-800-420-6088
www.globalsugarart.com

*Online store for all baking
and cake decorating supplies,
including edible food coloring
pastes, edible glitter, gum paste,
icings, and piping gel.*

N.Y. Cake & Baking Distributor
56 West 22nd Street
NY, NY 10021
Tel. 212-675-CAKE
www.nycake.com

*Online store for all baking
and cake decorating supplies,
including edible food coloring
pastes, edible dust and glitter,
icings, piping gel, and silicone
rubber push molds.*

Pfeil & Holing
Tel. 1-800-247-7955
www.cakedeco.com

*Online store for baking and cake
decorating supplies.*

Squires Kitchen
3 Waverley Lane
Farnham
Surrey GU9 8BB
UK
www.squires-shop.com
Tel. 011 44 1252 260260

*International supplier of silicone
rubber push molds; snowflake,
flower and holly leaf-shaped
plunger cutters; ready-made
icings and pastes; edible gold
leaf and edible confectioners'
glaze.*

Sweet Factory
Tel: 562-391-2410
www.sweetfactory.com

*Online store for all types of
candies.*

Wilton Homewares Store
Tel. 1-800-794-5866
www.wilton.com

*Online store for baking and cake
decorating supplies.*

USEFUL
CONTACTS

ACKNOWLEDGMENTS

Thanks to my mom for her baking and getting me hooked on cookies and cakes.

To Elizabeth Hurley for introducing me to Eric who has made my wilder dreams taste better than I could ever imagine.

A special thanks to Elton and David for writing the kind foreword to this book.

I would also like to thank our wonderful teams in the shop and bakery. Their boundless enthusiasm and hard work has been a big part of Cox Cookies & Cake's success.

Patrick Cox

Thank you to my first teachers Hervé Le Grand and Albert Roux— generous-hearted chefs who were happy to share their passion and their recipes…a spirit I hope to continue with my books and in my own Cookery School at Cake Boy.

To Paul for his unconditional support.

To Elizabeth for the introduction, and to Patrick for inviting me to join him on this exciting journey.

To all the staff at Cox Cookies & Cake and Cake Boy, and to Anne Kibel and Jean Egbunike.

To Rachel Wood and Wendy Lee for testing all our yummy recipes.

To Sybella, Juliette, and Jonathan for making this book so special.

To Becca—nice to work together again and I'm looking forward to the next project.

And finally a big thank you to Patrick Llewlyn-Davies for the amazing photography of the cakes.

Eric Lanlard

COOKIES & CAKE

Tattoo & Piercing

Ed's

Easy Diner

FULLY AIR CONDITIONED

KETTNERS

I kept wanting to